The Positive Perspective

Copyright © 2021 Nat Barouch

All rights reserved. No part of this publication may be reproduced, distributed, or transmitted in any form or by any means, including photocopying, recording, or other electronic or mechanical methods, without the prior written permission of the publisher, except in the case of brief quotations embodied in critical reviews and certain other noncommercial uses permitted by copyright law. For permission requests, contact Nat Barouch nat@bepositivepodcast.com

Any references to historical events, real people, or real places are used with permission.

Cover design - Nat Barouch
Cover photo - 123rf.com

Printed in the United States of America
First edition 3/2021

Nat Barouch
nat@bepositivepodcast.com
Morgantown WV, 26508

BePositivePodcast.com

Introduction

Nat is a happy guy. Most of us aren't. What's his secret?

He reveals it in this book, his first. He admits that he had a happy upbringing, but he also explains that what he knows can help the rest of us.

He regularly shares his experience and wisdom in his podcast. That's where I met Nat. He records upbeat messages, reminders, and more, including interviewing people like me, all to help the rest of us achieve what we all secretly want - happiness.

But he's now gone beyond his podcast and written this book. He's trying to help as many people as possible achieve what he has - inner peace.

You're in for a treat. There is joy, wisdom and more in these pages. I think you will read it, ponder, reflect, and finally achieve -- happiness.

Thoreau said most people lead lives of quiet desperation. Thoreau would approve of this book, as it's a remedy for misery.

Expect Miracles.
Dr. Joe Vitale
Author of way too many people to list here
A star in the hit movie The Secret

DEDICATION

This book is dedicated to my wife Jennifer who has always believed in me and given me the strength to be a better man, and has the courage to always do what's right. To my daughter Hope, who has listened to my rants and laughed at most of my jokes. Also to my son Nathan, may he become the man I know he can be.

I've never been a person to sit down and read a book, let alone write one but I felt compelled to publish this book. I have always been a very positive person. As long as I can remember, I felt the need to make people smile, even at my own expense. As a child my family life was no less than perfect. My family made enough money to get by but we were not wealthy by a long shot, but we were always happy. So many times we would all laugh together, go to the store together and go watch my dads band. We did everything together, life was great.

When my father passed away right before my 11th birthday my mom and I were devastated. I was mad at God for taking my dad and my mom was so depressed she did absolutely nothing for a year or two. Her mom, my grandmother, came to live with us to help with the bills and to be with my mom. Eventually my mom got the strength to pick herself up and decided she had to go get a job. (Besides the insurance money was running out.) I started 7th grade never realizing the deep emotional baggage I was carrying because I still blamed the world and God for my father's death.

My mom eventually started her own business and did very well for many years. She was always a rock in front of me but I knew she had lost her true love and would never love again. I was her world and she did everything to make sure I was happy.

My mom and my drums were everything to me. You see, drums became my escape. My dad was a drummer and I had been playing since age three. I got really good on drums probably because I played every waking moment. It was my only way of connecting with my dad.

When I went to college things changed a bit. Let's just say I got off track… for many years to follow. I toured the country and played in most of the US. The bad part was I got very distant from my mother. It was no fault of hers, it was me. I was embarrassed of who I'd become. Yes, I was an asshole for quite a few years. I thought I was invincible and I got away with everything. My mom used to tell me "You could step in shit and come out smelling like a rose," and she was right.

When my son was born I was still so wrapped up in myself that he didn't get the total attention from me like I got from my mom. When he was 10, I separated from his mom and later moved to another state after my mom passed away. Loosing her was and still is devastating. I still carry her positivity, sarcasm and wit with me.

A few years later I married the woman that turned my life around, Jennifer. We had been great friends for many years and I always had feelings for her. Her no BS attitude and her independence was just what I needed. We soon had our little girl and named her Hope. Being married to your best friend and a person that loves you unconditionally is something I cherish.

So now here I am happy, healthy, successful and in love. So why am I writing this book? Because I see so many people that are unhappy and don't realize they are choosing unhappiness. I know the mind controls the body. I know how to be happy. I know how to find the positive in most situations and I want to share this with the world. Hopefully, through the stories in this book, you will find your key that will open your door to happiness.

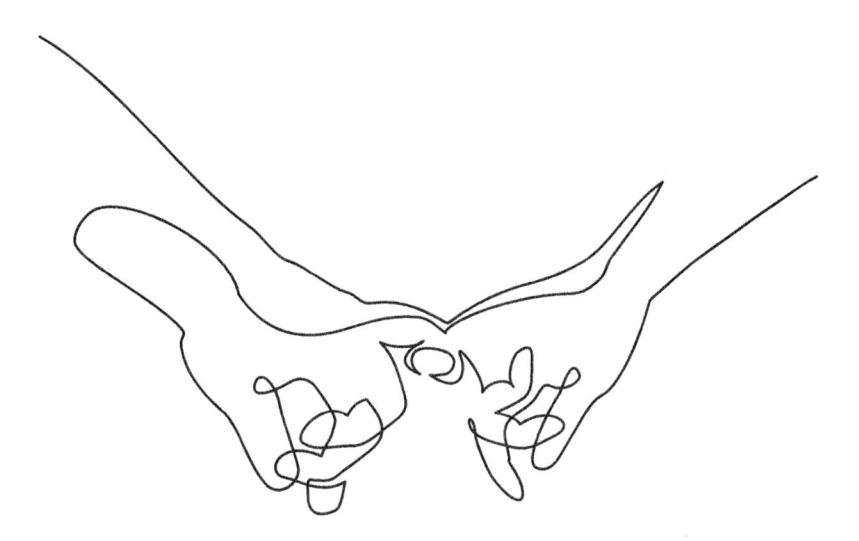

Your Beliefs	1
Your Mind Really Does Control Your Body	6
You Are Not Defined By Your Past	14
Can Gratitude Enhance Your Positivity?	20
Improve Your Willpower	24
What Are Emotional Alibis?	30
You Can Control Your Anger	38
Change Your Life With The 21-90 Rule	43
What If You Knew Your Future?	48
Leaving Your Comfort Zone Behind	54
How Important Are Material Things?	59
Your Inner Voice Doesn't Lie	63
Teaching Positivity To Your Children	69
Staying Positive With Willpower	74
Dealing With Medical Issues?	80
Negative Thoughts Ruin Your Life?	84
Believe In Your Passion	90
Extreme Emotions	94
Keeping Relationships Positive	99
Digital Friends vs Real Life	102
Remain In The Present	108
Keeping A Positive Mindset	112
Becoming Aware Of Negative Thoughts	117
Treating Friends Right	125
Put Your Past Behind You	130
Dealing With Internal Judgment?	134
Rejection Sucks	138
Your Last Day On Earth	142
Success = Happiness? Not Always	146
Think Positive Everyday	150
Have You Made The Right Choice?	155
Infinite Intelligence	160

~ The Positive Perspective ~

Chapter 1

Your Beliefs

What are your beliefs and why do you believe them? You probably believe them because that's what you were taught. They are engrained in your subconscious mind. You may not even know why you believe what you believe. Most of us never question our beliefs. Things like the religion you believe in. What is your definition of success? What type of partner you should have? The job you should have. Why do you believe these things? If you question why you believe something you might find out that you really don't believe it for the reasons you think you should.

You should believe something because it's true to you. Not because it's something your parents taught you or because it's what society expects of you. You should believe in things because you truly believe in them.

A lot of our beliefs are learned or inherited from what we were taught as children. Our parents instilled their beliefs in our fresh, un-programmed subconscious minds. Your mind is easily programmed when you are young but much more difficult to change when you get older. The things you are taught as a child are the things that you tend to believe.

Maybe you believe you should be more successful or have more in life. Maybe you don't have the things you want because you don't believe you deserve them or your beliefs are keeping you from them. If you were told life is hard, money doesn't grow on trees, great success is out of your reach you probably still believe that deep down in your subconscious.

So what do you do? Sit down and really analyze what you believe spiritually and emotionally. Validate your beliefs so you can be confident they are YOURS! If you cannot prove to yourself that you really believe in something, it's time to figure out why and change your belief.

Why are you where you are in life? It's because of the decisions you've made along the way. It's what you've been told to believe? Examine your beliefs, examine all your beliefs, religious, political, emotional or whatever it is that causes you to make the decisions in your life that you're making.

Stop and think why are you making those decisions? Why are you still working at a job if you're not happy? Why are you not doing what you love to do?

If you want abundance or great success, you've got to take a risk. Maybe you don't want to take a chance or take a risk because you are comfortable in your situation. Being comfortable plays a huge role in your belief system. Normally people don't want to challenge or go against their beliefs to take a risk on something different because they're afraid of the unknown. "I'm not going to rock the boat. I'm going to do what I've always done and just be comfortable in my situation and comfortable with my life."

~ The Positive Perspective ~

If that's the case and you're happy with where you are in life that's great. But if you're not happy, you have to understand what you have to do to change your life. How do you change your life? Simple, you change your way of thinking. You have to go against the grain and step out of the box and take some chances if you wish to accomplish more than the average person. Ninety-five percent of the people in the world are just complacent and happy with where they are in life. They are not willing to change their way of thinking because they've always thought that way.

You can do what ever you really want to. You choose what to believe in. You can choose your beliefs and not the beliefs that you've learned over the course of your life. Those beliefs are just programs and like a computer the program can be rewritten. Your brain is the most advanced computer in the world. Your mind actually is creating your body and your environment. So why not change your thoughts, change your beliefs and make your life what you want it to be? You have to actually catch yourself when you are doing things out of habit. The things that are not moving you towards your goal. Stop and ask yourself, why am I doing this? Because of my beliefs? Because it's a habit? Because I'm used to it? Because it's comfortable?

If you know the outcome your life is going be the same. It's not going to change it's not going to get better. If you're OK with that, that's awesome. If you want your life to be very predictable knowing the outcome, always staying at an acceptable pace and not having anything change then that's great. But if you want to progress and have a better life, a happier future and a more abundant life you must analyze your beliefs. You must make sure that they are your beliefs 100 percent not the beliefs that you have been taught throughout your life. Then you can begin to move forward and have the life you desire. You must step into the unknown, the unpredictable.

> *Steve Jobs said it best:*
> *"You can't connect the dots going forward. You can only look back and connect the dots of your past so your future is what you make it."*

Isn't that profound? It's what you make it. It's up to you. If you stay with your learned beliefs and just go along for the ride, your future is already written. It's going to be the same thing today that it was yesterday.

But if you want more out of your life, if you want to enjoy your life and love life you've got to grab it by the horns. It's time to analyze your beliefs, make the change and actually control your thoughts. You must be aware of what you're thinking about. Your thoughts become things. I say it a lot and I try to do it all the time. It's very difficult even when you're going about your day at your job eight hours doing the same thing. Stop and think about what you're thinking about. Stop and ask yourself, am I thinking about my ultimate goal?

Are you aware of your thoughts? Are your thoughts helping you make progress or are you just going through the motions? Do you count the minutes till 5 o'clock so you can get off work and go home and have a beer? Then that's going to be your life.

You'll leave work, eat dinner, sit on the couch, and watch TV. Hopefully you'll realize you did not think about what you're thinking. You'll go to sleep at night not thinking about your thoughts and your future, your goals, your dreams and your beliefs do not change. You wake up the next day and you do it all over again and wonder why your life doesn't change?

It's like the hamster on the wheel just going around and around and around and never getting anywhere. I want more out of my life and I think you do too or you wouldn't be reading this book. So analyze yourself, be honest with yourself, think about your thoughts, think about your beliefs. Ask yourself why do I believe what I believe?

Don't be surprised if you're not happy with what you find. If you're being totally honest, you might not like what you discover, but you have to face it and take control of it. Then take action to change your beliefs so they benefit your life, your thoughts, your dreams and your goals.

No one can say anything about it. It's your life. You can have, do or be anything you want.

Chapter 2

Your Mind Really Does Control Your Body

I just want to cheer you up, keep you happy, put a smile on your face and give you a positive outlook on life. I know I can't do it alone. You have to do it on your own. But maybe I can help a little bit. You never know. You never know.

What is getting you down today? What did you let get to you that brought you down and made you have a mediocre day? Or did you not have a mediocre day. Did you have a fantastic day? If you did, bravo! You're doing the right thing you're living life. You're doing what we are here to do what we're put here to do. We're put here to learn how to love and how to enjoy life.

You know you're here to enjoy your life and if you're not it's your fault. I will say that forever it is your fault if you're not enjoying your life. I enjoy my life even in the bad times because I'm living. We get to experience this thing called life for a short period of time and then we move on to the next realm of reality whatever that is. If you're religious you go to heaven. If your you believe in aliens you go to another planet. If you don't believe in anything you just go to the earth.

Energy goes on and on forever, it can't be created or destroyed, so when you die you really don't die your energy goes on in some form or another. So this is one little plateau that we are sent here to learn and how to love and to enjoy life and to be happy. Your life is going to go by so fast and pretty soon you're going to look in the mirror and go shit I'm old. I didn't get to do the things I wanted to do and you can't blame anyone but yourself. You can't honestly say that someone stopped you from doing it because you can literally do whatever you want to do. You can do what ever you want to do if you want to walk down the street naked, you can do it. There's consequences that you have to deal with but you can literally do whatever you want to do.

You can be good. You can be bad. You can be happy you can be sad. (Hey, that rhymed. It's almost like a Dr. Seuss book).

I'm here to help you find the good stuff. Everybody wants the good stuff right? I've always wanted the good stuff and I still do. I feel I have the good stuff, why? Because I choose it because I create it. I create my environment and you can too. You just you have to practice. You can't just say oh I'm going to be happy without emotionalizing the feelings of happiness. You'll often hear me say just be happy and flip the switch. The usual response I get is I can't do that. It's just easy for you.

If you say you can't, you're right.
What you tell yourself is your truth.

I bet the first time you got on a bike you couldn't ride it either could you? First time you tried to stand up you couldn't walk.

~ The Positive Perspective ~

The first time you tried to do your new job you couldn't do that either right. The first time you do anything is always difficult. You have to create good habits. You have to practice. You have to control your mind. You have to control your body.

The fact is, your mind controls your body. If you convince your mind that you're happy, you're healthy, you believe it and you see it in your minds eye, it will become your personal reality.

I'd like to share a little story with you. I thought of an invention idea for a silverware organizer clip. I had no money and no way to make it happen. No thoughts of how I'm going to pull this off. But I was dead set on doing it and I said I'm going to make this happen. So I raised the money with Kickstarter. Then I learned how to use 3D software. I created my prototypes on a little 300 dollar 3D printer, perfected my design and got it manufactured. I designed the packaging, got the UPC code and it was ready to sell. I didn't get rich but I sold a few and I did it because I was relentless with my dream. I remained positive even when it looked like it was pointless. My positive thoughts kept me going but it works both ways.

If you are constantly down and constantly focusing on being depressed and focusing on what's bad and saying I have all these bills and no money to pay them. I hate my job or my relationship is terrible. Traffic is bad, people are awful. If you constantly think about the negative, that's all you're going to see. It's going to feed on itself and bring more negative things into your life.

I'm perpetually happy. Sure there's times that I'm not happy of course, everyone has times in their lives that are unhappy or depressed. It's how you deal with those emotions that really matter. I'm happy because I choose to be happy. Some people think I'm crazy or I'm faking it. They say how can you be so happy all the time? It can't be real you must be putting on a show. To that I say why are you so unhappy all the time? Your life can't really be that bad. I think your overreacting and putting on a show. People don't like that. Then I explain to them that both positive and negative emotions are all controlled by the same thing... YOU!

I often wonder why it is ok for people to be upset and depressed but when someone is happy "they're up to something". I really make my life this simple. I am thankful every morning because I got to wake up again. It's that simple. It really is. When you start your day with complaining or negativity that sets the course for the rest of the day. You will attract everything you think about. One day you're not going to wake up or you're going be sick and not be able to do anything. Then you'll say I wish I would have been happier. I wish I would have followed my heart.

You've got to get out and do the things you want to do. You must take control of your life, of your thoughts. Your mind controls your body don't let your environment control your mind. Don't let your situation dictate how you think because it's unhealthy. It's not the way it's supposed to be.

You are the creator of your life and your world, whether you believe it or not.

~ The Positive Perspective ~

People have said to me wow things just come your way. Everything just falls in your lap. It brings to mind a saying I used to hear a lot growing up, "Nat can step in a pile of crap and come out smelling like a rose." Now I realize it is true. Why? Because I do not let the negative things dictate my life. I turn them into positive situations. I believe, I honestly believe good things will come to me and they do. You're probably thinking yeah right you just think good things and they just come into your life. Well, that is not 100% correct. Bad things come into my life just like everyone else. It's how I choose to deal with them that creates the open door for good to come in.

A lot of this has to do with the way you present yourself and the way you feel about the universe as a whole. I think we're all connected and I use that to my advantage. I try to help people by teaching them how to help themselves or by pointing out things that make them feel better. Sometimes I do something that will cheer them up. That's just me, it's just the way I am. Just know not everybody is alike. At least that's what my daughter keeps telling me.

The world is full of an immeasurable amount of personalities. Some people like to be depressed or negative because they get attention. They don't take the time to realize they are actually creating depressing lives by letting the outside chatter dictate the way they perceive the situation.

Let's say you're depressed because you're broke. You constantly tell people you have no money. It's not your fault, it's because of where you live, your parents, your x-boss. Remember YOU are in control of your thoughts. You are in control of your actions. You are in control of your life. So why are you broke? Because YOU are not taking action to become financially stable. Your excuse is _____ (fill in the blank with your personal excuse). Then realize it IS an excuse and get moving and create something do something productive. Think about how to add something to this world instead of feeling like you're entitled to something. The world and the people in it *owe you nothing.*

Don't just sit there wallow in your own self pity because you don't have something or don't have a job. Maybe you got fired. Well, then why don't you go get another job. Maybe your wife or your girlfriend left you. Ask yourself why. If you are living an honest life and being true to yourself then move on. But you know things that happen to you nine times out of ten are your fault. Address the situation and figure out the solution. Of course there are unforeseen incidents or accidents that happen that are out of your control. The way you choose to deal with them makes all the difference. Choose to be negative and dwell on your misfortune and you will attract more of the same negativity. Choose to put a positive spin on it and try to find the good and that will also attract the good to you.

I don't believe that accidents like falling off a ladder getting in a car accident are actually brought on by you. But if you are sick and you always talking about being sick, and focusing on being sick you will continue to be sick or get sicker. Letting your body deteriorate and focusing on the disease that you have attracted more of the same. Laugh, be happy, focus on the good in your life and you will be less sick.

When you say I can't do it or I can't change, you are correct. When you say I can do it and I can change you are also correct.

~ The Positive Perspective ~

Two very powerful words are I can!

You have to go on with life because one day you're not gonna have it. The chances of you becoming a human being are like 4 billion to one. So when you are thankful for every day and you believe this life is a gift, it will open your life to so many possibilities it will amaze you. The gratitude you put out there will be rewarded.

If you've had a near-death experience or something that has made you think *wow that could have taken my life in a whole different direction or maybe ended it,* you start to think, I'm so lucky that didn't happen. After that it becomes easier for you to be positive and stay positive. But if you've already fallen into that slump to where something has taken away all your hope, maybe you're in a wheelchair or you're terminally ill and you focus on that, you will never be happy.

Ok this might be a bit morbid right now, but here goes. Let's say you have a terminal illness and you know you're going to die. *Kind of a nasty turn here but go with me on this it sets a good example.* What would you do with your life? Would you feel sad? Sure. Of course you'd be upset but if you focus on the fact you're going to die you'll probably remain depressed and ask yourself why me? But after that you need to accept it and move forward and live the rest of your life to the fullest. Guess what? We're all going to die! Most of us just don't know when. Remember we are all energy. Energy can't be created or destroyed. So the only part that is actually dying is your psychical body. Your spirit and energy will go on forever.

~ The Positive Perspective ~

Staying positive is going to get you through the roughest times of your life. It's going to make you feel better about yourself. It's gonna give you the energy to go on, to be a better person, to help other people. It will enable you to leave your mark on the world in a positive way.

So it's up to you. I'll give you the key to the door but you have to open it.

Chapter 3

You Are Not Defined By Your Past

We've all made mistakes but when you say they are to blame for your future you are wrong. How can I say that with such conviction? Because what you did or what happened to you in your past is your past. Don't let your past dictate your future. Your future depends on the actions you take today and on the decisions you make now. Your thoughts, the way you project your positivity and the way you go through the next portion of your life will determine your future.

Think about that for a second. Every action, everything you do, everything you think and everything you say is creating your future. Remember, what you've done in your past has gotten you to the point that you're at now. Your future will be created by the actions and the thoughts that you take from this point on. So if you don't like where you are in the present, change it. Change your thoughts. Change the pictures in your mind. You <u>can</u> change the way you think.

You are where you are right now in life it because of the decisions you've made in the past.

If you keep doing the same thing over and over again and keep thinking the same thoughts you're going to end up in the same place a year from now, ten years from now twenty years from now it's not going to change unless you change. So you must change your thoughts and create new habits. Always make sure that you're keeping positive thoughts in your mind. As long as you're emulating positivity, you're paying it forward and you're having positive thoughts your life will get better. It has too. It's the law of attraction. It's a law of nature. It's the law of the universe.

Happy people, and I mean really happy not just in the photos they share on social media, usually stay that way because they practice happiness and positivity. I know, I'm one of the happy people. Maybe they've made mistakes in their past but they're not letting their past mistakes dictate their future. They learn from the mistakes. They move on and they go forward.

The old saying that the definition of insanity is doing the same thing over and over again and expecting a different outcome. So if you're doing the same things you've done most of your life and you're expecting your life to get better, guess what? It's not going to get better. It won't get better unless you change your thoughts and change the way you think. You have to change the way you look at things and really start appreciating your life.

Your life is a beautiful gift. What you make of it is totally your decision. You really have to appreciate your life. Appreciate yourself, be proud of yourself and stay positive about all the things in your life even when bad things happen. Practice gratitude by actually saying thank you over and over for everything in your life. Show gratitude for your family, the roof over your head, and the food in your refrigerator. I think when something bad happens something good usually comes out of that. Well, I don't know if that's always true, but it is a very optimistic way to look at things. You can always find the good in every situation if you look hard enough. Find the positive perspective. If you can't find the good, create it in your mind. Make something good come from that situation, turn the negative into a positive.

I began this chapter saying your future is not your past. You have to remember that you can't condemn your future because of what happened to you in the past. Many successful people have come from a broken home or an abusive childhood. Sure your past has created who you are today, but it doesn't have the power to keep you there unless you let it. You see, having the understanding that your past can't be changed is liberating. Knowing and believing you have the willpower to change your path in life with your thoughts may be hard to believe, but once you understand this, your life will change. Hold in your mind the vision of what you want your life to be. Every waking moment take action to reach your goals. Put the past away and look to your future.

I bet you're saying how can you do that how can you be happy and think all the way into the future? It's easy for you but I can't do it.

Remember whether you think you can or you think you can't, you are correct.

Imagine you're in a car and you're driving from New York to California at night. You can only see about 100 feet in front of you with the light from the headlights. But you know this road will take you to California. If you follow this road and you look for the next hundred feet and you just follow those lights and you follow that road you're going to eventually get to your destination.

Your life is like that too. You can't plan your future for the next 30 years, you have to just take it one step at a time and deal with what is directly in front of you. Just keep moving forward into your future creating your present. That's all you have to do. Think about the moment right in front of you, about your thoughts, stay positive and stay focused. Most importantly, keep those positive vibes going in your mind.

Don't dwell on your past because you can't change it. Your past does not dictate your future. Let me say that one more time your past does not dictate your future. What you're thinking now is what your future will be. The pictures you hold in your mind, your positive affirmations and everything you think about will help you to create a better life and to be happier.

I think everyone really wants to be a nice person but they blame their past for their negative actions. They think that it's a good enough excuse. It gives them a reason to be negative or to be self-destructive. Placing blame outside of yourself for any situation is just a cop out. You have control of your mind you have control of your body so you are in total control of your destiny.

~ The Positive Perspective ~

It may be hard to understand if you've been blaming your past for where you are right now in life. That's OK because you're reading this book so now you can make that change. You can accept the fact that your past decisions have gotten you to where you are today but you don't have to stay there. You can move forward by changing your thoughts.

Life was made to be abundant, energetic and full of joy. If you're not happy and you're not enjoying your life now is your chance to make the positive shift. I wish I could just come to your house and show you how to be happy, but I can't do that for you. No one can, it's up to you. Hopefully I can convince you that you have the power inside of you to make the changes that you want to make to live a better life. You have the power to push those negative thoughts out and fill your mind with positive thoughts about everything in your life.

If you don't like the situation you're in and you can't get out of it right away. Keep visualizing the new situation. Keep visualizing where you want to be and your life will change. You'll start finding ways to be happier and that's what this is all about. This book is about helping you to find the keys to your happiness. It's not about me telling you how to be happy. It's about me opening up your mind so you can control your own happiness. Once you get control of that and understand it, you will be a happier person.

But your goal is to control your mind, control your happiness and practice, practice, practice happiness, happy thoughts and positive thoughts. As soon as you feel that negative thought, replace it with a positive one. Get it out of there because that negative thought is going to hold you back. It's going to drag you down and keep you from the happy future that you so deserve

You're in control. You have total control of your mind. Think about it. You can do what ever you really want to do right. Sure there are consequences for some things but you can literally do what ever you want to do. If you want to quit your job you can do that. You'll be broke but you could do that if you want to walk across the United States, you can do that. People have done it. Whatever you really want to do and you put your mind to it you can do.

So why not put your mind into creating a better future for yourself through your positive thoughts.

Chapter 4

Can Gratitude Enhance Your Positivity?

Does gratitude actually contribute to your positivity and your happiness? Many people say there are so many benefits to being grateful and showing gratitude. I think it starts when you wake up. Start your day by being grateful that you woke up again. Sounds simple right? Think about this for a minute. One day you will not get to wake up and the physical part of your life will be over. That puts things in perspective right? So be grateful you have another day on this earth. Show gratitude for all the little things you normally take for granted. Be grateful that you can sit up, stand up, walk to the bathroom and brush your teeth. Feeling gratitude for these little things, and realizing it's all a gift, will help you to appreciate the things you do have and all the things you can do. Let's examine what gratitude does for your life and your positivity.

The benefits of gratitude.

Well, first of all, gratitude makes you a happier person. You will experience much more happiness when you're grateful for everything in your life. You'll have more good feelings and you're more relaxed. You won't let little things stress you out and you're grateful for all the things that come your way in your life. (Especially when you understand you are the creator of your life.) You can even be grateful for ordering fast food and finally getting exactly what you ordered. (Like that really happens.) Be grateful that you have a job that pays your bills. Show gratitude towards the people that love you. Be grateful that your car started this morning. Make it that easy. Gratitude leads to emotional happiness and positivity.

So the benefits of gratitude, on an emotional level, give you a better feeling about yourself. You're more relaxed, you're more resilient & you're less envious of other people.

How does gratitude affect your personality?

It makes you less materialistic because you're thankful for the things that you have, even all the little things. You're more optimistic, more spiritual and you'll have more faith in your goals and dreams. It also helps to increase your self-esteem. So your overall personality will benefit from you being grateful for everything in your life. You're healthier when you're grateful because of the positive energy flowing through your body. Being grateful will also improve your sleep. Yet another bonus is you won't get sick as often because you're grateful for your health. You're going to live longer because you're not going to be stressed. It's a known fact that stress, in any form, reduces your life. It diminishes your positive energy causing cells to breakdown.

You'll have a healthier marriage if you're grateful for it and you show gratitude towards your spouse. They will be so happy and it'll make for a happy household and a happier life. We've all heard happy wife, happy life or happy spouse, happy house.

So does gratitude enhance your positivity? Yes, it absolutely does on a spiritual level and on a personal level. You'll have more friends your marriage will be better your career will be better all because you're grateful for the things you have. When you're grateful, when you have that attitude of gratitude, it shows in everything you do.

So what if you don't feel gratitude?

What if you can't find or think of something to be grateful for? What if you are one of those people that says oh my life is miserable, I hate my job, my health isn't great, I'm overweight or I live in a crappy place. What do I have to be grateful for?

First of all you need to be grateful that you live in a time where you have access to instant information form all over the planet. You can be thankful that you are reading this book and have eyes to do so. Do you see a roof over your head? I bet you do. You should be thankful for that. No matter how you're keeping that roof over your head be thankful that you have shelter, food, your health, your family and your friends. Being grateful is more than just saying thank you. Being grateful is a spiritual feeling deep inside. It's a warmth. It's a satisfaction that is so huge it's hard to put into words. You may feel like you do not deserve everything that you have. Being grateful for what you do have, paying it forward by helping other people get what they want and making other people's life better is also a great feeling. You can make someone's life better just by being grateful, actually sharing the positivity through gratitude by being grateful for something that someone else does for you.

You're actually making them feel positive about the contribution that they're making to the world.

So we're going to start one person at a time. Your task is to be grateful and say thank you for the things that you have in your life. Write them down, make a list. Make it simple and put everything you can think of on this list. Even if it's simple and sounds silly to write it down, do it anyway. Then look at it and remember there are people out there that don't have the things that you have. They don't have the health, the roof over their head, the refrigerator full of food or even shoes, so be grateful for everything that you have.

If you've got too much stuff laying around, donate it. It will help someone else's life to be better and you'll feel good about yourself as well. You'll also reduce your clutter and have a cleaner house, which is something my wife would love me to do.

So what about the attitude of gratitude and does it enhance your positivity? It absolutely does and it makes you feel good when you're grateful and you realize all the good stuff you have in your life and be thankful for it.

Positivity will open the door to your happiness. Trust me it works.

Chapter 5

Improve Your Willpower

Willpower is one thing that many people do not have enough of. Most of the population gives up when the going gets tough. When something gets difficult, we find it easier to give up and move onto something easier. So how can you improve your willpower?

Wherever possible remove all the temptations from your life that keep you from using your willpower. For example if you know that you watch too much TV but you need to focus on a project, do your homework, or take care of some business then turn the TV off.

Step away from the TV, unplug it if necessary. I know I eat junk food if it's in the house. So I try not to keep it in the house, but when it's here I'll eat it. I don't have the willpower to not eat the junk food so I have to get it out of my sight. If you have an addiction you have to get away from the people and the environment that enables your addiction. Remove the temptation; this will help improve your willpower. It works. Trust me.

Make sure you get enough sleep. Research has shown that the ability to maintain focus on tasks suffers due to a lack of sleep.

If you're not getting enough sleep you can't focus. Different people need different amount of sleep to be fully functional. I know people that sleep for four hours a night and they're fine. I'm one of them, for about 4 days then I need a good 8.

So if you need four, if you need six, if you need eight, whatever you need, get quality sleep so you can be sharp when you are awake. That way you can focus on your tasks and have the willpower to stick to them and follow through.

Enjoy your life, sounds simple right? This will help your willpower. Positive emotional experiences replenish your self-discipline reserve. It will give you more willpower. So throughout the day take a few moments to enjoy your life. Stop and smell the flowers (to use an old saying). Take breaks and do the things that make you feel good and help you enjoy your life. To me I like to play my drums, I like to shoot and edit video and I love doing my Be Positive Podcast.

So do what you love and enjoy your life. It will give you the strength you need to tap into your willpower.

Reduce the stress in your life. Stress will wear you down and make you give up. It doesn't give you the strength to have willpower. So how can you reduce stress? Reduce your commitments; do some breathing exercises, maybe yoga will help you relax.

Do the things that you love. Sit down and pet your cat. (*I say that a lot. I'm not a big cat lover but maybe you are so pet your cat, pet your dog, or even pet your turtle...*) Go fishing or just sit on your patio and look outside at Mother Nature's beauty. Whatever you can do to avoid and reduce stress will be beneficial.

Listen to some soft music. You can go to your favorite online streaming service and find music that will help move you into a very relaxed state. Get away from the people and the situations that stress you out.

Research shows that when your willpower starts getting depleted, having a plan helps keep you on track. You've got a vision of the life you want to have. If you really have a burning desire to follow your dream whether it's to make a lot of money, to get a better job, to get a new person in your life, or to get a new car. Whatever it is, the willpower you need to get to that state is going to be strengthened.

You must have a plan on how to get there. You just can't say, "Oh, I want a new house" and not have a plan on how to get it. You must work for it because nothing comes for free.

But remember, you always have to give something to get something. So you'll have to give some of your time to make the money or you'll have to give something in order to get what you need. You have to have that burning desire to follow through with your plan. If it fails, revise it, regroup and move forward.

I've been talking about this for a long time. Your plan has to become a habit in order for you to achieve it. You have to have the willpower to get through failure, which is not really a failure. When you fail, you learn from your mistakes and you get closer to success.

*I don't look at failure as failure.
I look at it as one step closer to success.*

Even if you start all over, you are starting with experience. So have a plan to reach your goal and have the willpower to follow through with it.

Positive affirmations have been shown to help replenish your depleted willpower. When you start to get weak, talk to yourself. Positive self talk is as impactful as negative self talk. You control it. The more you do it the more your subconscious mind will accept it and bring it into your reality.

Talk to yourself and tell yourself positive things that you want to do. Visualize your end goal, where you want to go and the things you want to accomplish. See that lifestyle that you want to live in your mind and use that as the strength for your willpower to be stronger to follow through with your dreams. Above all, never give up at the first sign of difficulty. You have to continually program yourself and fill your mind with positive thoughts and positive affirmations and remember all of the things that you will achieve when you get to your goals. It gives you the willpower to keep going forward and to keep striving to achieve the things that you want to achieve.

Having willpower is not a difficult thing, it is learned behavior. The more you use it, the more it becomes second nature to you. By doing it over and over again and keeping what you want to accomplish in your mind at all times you'll find the strength to have the willpower. You just have to really want to. You have to have that burning desire in order to achieve your goals.

~ The Positive Perspective ~

Now here's a little bonus tip for you just from my mind to yours if you're trying to build your willpower.

Think about this: Willpower is hard. Yes, being a success is hard. Yes, doing things that you don't want to do because you're being told to do them is hard. But think about successful, happy people. Do you think everything was always easy for them? Do you think they did not have willpower and didn't push through the rough times in order to get to where they are now? Do you think that everything just came easy and they did not have to work for it? Willpower gives you strength; it gives you confidence and helps you focus on where you're headed in life.

If you keep your goals in focus and keep that burning desire alive you'll have more willpower. Now maybe you're burning desire isn't burning enough to get you fired up. Remember only you can change that.

I look at your desire like this. If you have small desire it's like little bit of fire and you get a little bit of heat, but if you have a burning desire and you really want to accomplish something it's your ultimate goal, you have a big fire and you have a lot of heat. That's what you need: A lot of heat and a lot of fire behind your goals and behind your dreams in order to accomplish them. To get that you've got to have that willpower strength and that willpower focus to accomplish your dream. You got this.

~ The Positive Perspective ~

Emotional Alibis Holding You Back
by Hope Barouch

Chapter 6

What Are Emotional Alibis?

Well, it's not something I just made up. Outside of that, emotional alibis are the things that we tell ourselves. They can hold us back. These are excuses for things you've not accomplished or changes you haven't made in your life.

> *They include thoughts like:*
> *"If I only had enough money, I could have done that."*
> *"If I only met the right person, I'd be happy."*
> *"If it was only the right time to make a change."*

These are just a few examples of some excuses people constantly tell themselves. But the fact remains that you are exactly where you are in life because of the decisions you've made. Think about that one for a second. That's why you're where you are... because of the decisions that you have made in your life.

That's crazy when you really think about it. But, if you analyze yourself and accept yourself 100 percent for who you are, the decisions and mistakes you've made as well as the accomplishments you've achieved, then you realize that you're where you're at right now because of the decisions you've made in your past.

You are the creator of your life.

The good news is you don't have to stay there because your past is your past and your future is what you make it. It really works that way. Your future will change with every decision you make today, tomorrow, the next day, next week, next month, next year. With every decision, your life takes a different course. You have to make those decisions with confidence. You have to know why you're making decisions and always be working toward your outcome, your final goal. Whether it's to be in a happy relationship, whether it's to have an awesome job that you love, whether it's to live in a different part of the world, whether it is to make a YouTube channel or whether it's to have a podcast.

Do it all the way and never give up!

Many people are going to react negatively towards your thoughts, dreams and goals because they're not fulfilling theirs. Subconsciously they want to bring you down and refuse to believe that your goals are realistic. But if you think about this for a second, your subconscious does not know the difference between reality and fantasy. It does not know whether your goal is tangible, whether it's real or if it's not, it just doesn't know.

So, for example, if you tell your subconscious over and over and you keep visualizing in your mind that you're going to make $10,000 within one year and you don't know how you're going to do it, but you convince yourself and you believe it and you see it, your subconscious is going to do everything in its power to make it happen. It has to because that's its job.

You have to make decisions in your life and you have to get rid of your emotional alibis. How do you do that? You do that by facing each one. When you say, "Oh, I would like to have a bigger house if I only had more money," that's probably a fact, but that's also an excuse. If you want a bigger house, find a way to make more money.

You may not be getting rich off of your job. If you're in a 9-to-5 job and you have a salary, you're making a certain amount of money. You're probably not going to become a millionaire. Most of the people who have a job are not going to become millionaires from that job. You have to supplement your income with multiple sources of income, (but that's a whole other book).

If it's your goal to have a bigger house, a newer car, or you want to travel, find ways to do it. You don't have to be rich to do things you just have to plan and stick to a budget. You don't have to have money to be happy.

You have to face yourself realistically and analyze all aspects of your life, all of your emotional alibis, all of your excuses, all of the reasons that you say you're not where you want to be in life. Write them down. I'm not successful because my job doesn't pay me enough money. Okay. You're blaming the job, but you chose that job and you're working at that job. If you're not happy with the money you're making or the actual job, find a way to get a better job.

If you need more education, get the education so you can make more money. Find a way to get what you want. Don't make the excuses for things you don't have because it's ultimately your fault. It really is.

When you say, wow, I really want to do this, you have to jump on it and act on it right away.

Life is like a checkerboard and the opposing player is time.

If you hesitate or fail to move promptly, your will be wiped off the board. You don't have enough time to wait for the "right time" to do everything. It will NEVER be the "right time". Maybe you're thinking, it's not the right time to take this vacation. Yes, it is. You thought about it, you dreamed of it and you want to do it. So make it happen. Do it! You think it's not the right time to start a new job. You say, I don't think I can afford it. Well, if you don't think you can afford it, you can't. If you don't think you should, then you won't. You won't.

If you think you can, you can.
If you think you can't, you can't.

Let's go off topic for a moment. In the past, I've gotten burned out by all the things I do in my off time. I try to balance everything. You can quickly burn out if you try to do too much and you're not organized and not focused. It's like when you spin a top on the table and right before it falls it gets all wobbly and crazy. You'll get that way if you don't stay in control and stay focused. You have to control your thoughts and don't let them run wild. I've let thoughts wander before. It took all I had to get back on track. I usually go into the studio and record a podcast.

Time is always going to win. When you feel like you've got to do something, when you have that inspiration about something, act on it. Don't think about it so much to where you overthink it and you freak yourself out and don't do it. You'll create the negativity and you won't do it. You have to control the negativity. You have to always block the outside negativity because it will fuel your emotional alibis. When you say, I want to go on a vacation, but people say you can't afford that. Don't accept someone else dictating your life and telling you what you can and can't do. You do what you want to do, what you need to do to be you.

Because like I said in the beginning of this chapter…where you are in life is where you want to be because you've made the decisions to get you to this point. Good or bad, you've made all of your decisions yourself. Now, you might say it's because of my situation. I didn't have control of my situation. There are just so many excuses. That's your emotional alibi's making it okay for you to fail.

Don't fail at your life. If you're not doing what you love, living life to the fullest, then you're wasting this gift of life that you've been given. Life is a gift.

You're here to learn how to love. You're here to enjoy this little part of your existence. So enjoy it. Enjoy it. Don't get old and say, I wish I had done this, but I didn't because I was married to someone who wouldn't let me. I couldn't do that because the job wouldn't let me leave. Those are called emotional alibis. That's your personal excuse to make it okay and make you not accept your own decisions.

I'm working through my own emotional alibis. I am facing them and saying, "Okay, I know where I'm at right now. I am happy where I'm at right now. I'm content with all of my decisions that I've made to get me to this point, but I don't want to stay at this point. I've got some goals that I have set for myself. I've got things that I want to accomplish in the next year and the next five years."

Write down your goals and put them where you can see them every single day. Here are my goals. Here's what I want to accomplish this year. Look at it in the morning. Read it out loud.

Sometimes people try to bring me down into negativity. Sometimes I give in and I get upset and pissed off and let it bring me down. If it lasts for more than two minutes, once I come out of it, I am like, damn, then I ask myself, "Why was I mad?" I was mad at what somebody else said. Why do I let them get to me? So I constantly, **stop and think about what I'm thinking about.**

Think about what you're thinking about and plant the positive seeds in your mind's garden. Then weed out the emotional alibis.

Don't let your excuses dictate your life. Don't let your life run you. You run your life. You make your decisions. You control your thoughts. Your thoughts control your life. Your thoughts create the pictures of your life. Become the director of your life every day. You must tell yourself you're going to have a good day, and then insist on having a good day and don't let things get to you. Sometimes it works, right? Well, the more you do it, the easier it gets and the more of a habit it becomes. And then you're happy all the time and everybody says you're crazy! But that's okay because you're happy. That's why we're here.

We're here to be happy.
We're here to enjoy our life.

So here's what I want you to do. Next time you make an excuse for something, why you don't have something, why you can't go somewhere, why you're not doing something? Stop and think…is it really something on the outside that is stopping you? Or is it the fact that you haven't taken the risk or taken the chance or figured out a way to do it yourself?

If you're really honest with yourself, you'll realize that you can really do whatever you want. You absolutely can. The whole world is yours. Every single person in the world can do what they want if they believe in themselves. That's why we have rich people, inventors, pilots, artists, musicians etcetera. Because that's what they wanted to do and they said they're going to do it no matter what. That's what you've got to do. Get rid of the emotional baggage. Get rid of those emotional alibis. Throw them out. Face up to them and realize that you're making excuses for your life. Don't make excuses for your life. Embrace where you are. Write down your goals of where you want to go. Figure out how you're going to get there and take steps to better your life. Because we're here to enjoy it, and before you know it that checkerboard is going to be empty and time's going to run out. All of your game pieces are going to be gone.

I'm going for the king. I'm getting crowned, and I'm going to win this checker game of life and you should too. Take life by the horns. Come on. Let's do it. Let's enjoy the crap out of this life and do and have a great life and make life fun. It's your life. It should be fun. And it can be fun if you make it fun.

Don't let somebody else ruin your life because, in the end, the only person that's going to suffer is you. So don't do it.

Chapter 7

You Can Control Your Anger

We're digging into your mind, digging into life, digging into things that really mess with you or can really hinder your happy, positive life. Anger is one of those things.

I am mad! Not really. I'm not really mad. I don't get mad a lot. Maybe you think have anger issues? Do you find it difficult to control emotions? I received a letter from someone who lives in Norway. She said she has issues with her anger. Many people get so worked up and so mad they cannot control their emotions. They get provoked so easily and it's hard for them to not be angry. So how do you control your anger?

First, try your best to stay away from the things that make you mad. If you can't do that, here's a few ways to become aware of your emotions and control them. Stop and take a breather. What do I mean by that? When you're angry, your breathing becomes shallower, and it begins to speed up. You'll notice you start breathing really fast when you get mad. To counter this, practice the reverse: Take slow, deep breaths through your nose. Exhale out of your mouth for several minutes to calm yourself.

As you focus on your breathing, you'll become aware of the anger and realize it's a controllable emotion.

While you're doing that, walk around to help reduce your anger. Exercise calms your nerves and reduces your anger level. Go for a walk, get away from what's angering you. Ride your bike, hit some golf balls, or play tennis. Anything that gets your arms and legs pumping is good for your mind and your body. It will help you to control that anger.

As my grandmother used to say: "Don't get mad; only dogs get mad." It's really not useful, in my mind, to get angry and totally upset and furious. When you are angry, you end up saying things that you regret and you hurt people that you love. Then you have to apologize for it. After which you look at yourself and say: "Man that was stupid. Why did I get angry?" After all of that the situation that caused your anger hasn't changed. It's still there even after you've calmed down. So the end result is that all you've done is to get yourself worked up and angry for no reason. You still have to deal with the situation. You can handle the issue much better by staying calm and clearly evaluating the problem.

Something else I like to do is mentally escape. Go into a quiet room and close your eyes. Practice visualizing yourself in a relaxing scene. Take yourself away to a beach scene where or to somewhere that you find totally relaxing. Maybe it's just sitting on your patio sipping a margarita with the birds chirping in your backyard. Whatever it is. Take yourself there in your mind. Visualize yourself escaping into your own world.

~ The Positive Perspective ~

Practice this and you will find yourself actually distancing yourself from your anger. It will dissipate allowing you to be more relaxed and able to approach the situation with a more open mind. Another method is to play some music you enjoy. Let the music carry you away from the anger. Put some earbuds in and crank up your favorite tunes. You may not want to break out Metallica or anything like that. But if that's your favorite music and dissipates your anger then go for it. Your anger will dissolve because it's music that you love. (For me, it would have to be Boston.) Find the music that makes you relax.

The next tip may be difficult for some: Stop talking. Just stop talking! When you are upset or and you're pissed off, you'll be tempted to let angry words fly. You're going to say things that you will regret later. You're likely to do more harm than good. The anger is going to escalate; it's going to feed off of itself. It's not going to be resolved unless you STOP TALKING! Pretend that your lips are glued shut just like you did when you were a kid. Mouths shut. Ears open. Right? So keep your mouth shut. Talking will cause you to dig yourself in deeper. When you stop talking, you will have time to collect your thoughts, to think about the issue that caused your anger. Not talking is giving you a time out. Give yourself a break. It's okay to be quiet. Take a personal time out and walk away from the situation. You can then process the events in a logical frame of mind without being angry, allow your emotions to return to a neutral state and get back to that positive energy that we're all seeking. You will find this time away to be very helpful.

Do it more often. Getting away from people can be very helpful in other ways to really diffuse your anger, to really get a grip on it, to not get provoked and go crazy. Remind yourself to be grateful. Practice your gratitude...like I have talked about on the Be Positive Podcast. Think about all the good things you have in your life. Is it worth getting angry over this situation? Take a moment to focus on what's right when everything feels wrong. Realize how many good things you have in your life that can help you neutralize your anger and turn the situation around, just by practicing gratitude. It's an amazing emotion and it will help you get through your anger. Be thankful for what you have as well as the person you are angry with. Examine why this person is in your life? Why am I arguing with them? Most likely you have a strong bond with them. It's often not worth the argument. Life is too short to argue with someone over things that aren't worth it.

Think about this for a second. You're angry with someone and they're angry with you. The conversation is getting heated. What if you step out of your shoes and step into the other person's shoes and see the situation from their perspective? When you view the events *as they see it*, you may develop a new understanding and become less angry. You're now seeing the story from their side, from their perspective. So maybe if you see yourself through someone else's eyes, you might realize you were angry for a silly or easily resolved reason. Find that positive perspective.

Okay, here's one additional quick tip. Express your anger. It's okay to say how you feel as long as you handle it the right way. Outbursts and angry words are not the way to express your anger. A mature dialogue can reduce your stress and ease your anger, and it just might prevent future problems and help you smile a little more.

Chapter 8

Change Your Life With The 21-90 Rule

So what is the 21-90 rule? The 21-90 rule means it takes 21 days to build or break a habit, and 90 days to create a lifestyle. This means if you can do something for 21 days straight you'll break (or build) a habit. Let's assume you want to quit smoking, for example, and you manage to make it through 21 days without smoking. You've broken that habit after 21 days and now you want to make it a lasting lifestyle. You must maintain it for 90 days to create the lifestyle. That's what this chapter is about.

It is also about changing your life using the 21-90 rule. It will help you change and make a shift in your daily life…whether it's being more fit, getting stronger, or eating better. We all want to do little things that make us happier and make us feel better, but we find it difficult to do. The 21-90 rule might work for you. So how can you implement this into your life?

The first thing is to identify the habit that you wish to break. Something in your life that you want to change. Maybe you are reading this book because you're missing something in your life. Perhaps you're feeling like there's more out there for you. Maybe, just maybe, this book is going to give you the key that opens the door to your happiness. It may help you

~ The Positive Perspective ~

understand what's going on inside of you and help you become a happier, more productive person. The whole goal of this book is to help you be happy with yourself.

Ok, let's focus on the habit that you either want to make or break. What do you want to start doing, or perhaps what do you want to stop doing? Sit down and think about what it is that you don't want to do anymore. Whether it's smoking, overeating, maybe it's drinking, maybe it's being mean to people, or maybe it's something you want to do such as start exercising.

You have to start by developing the willpower to do it, to get up off the couch and actually do it, and then commit to it every single day. Start out by doing it once. If you're trying not to over eat, push that food away more than once every day. Keep pushing it away and continue that for 21 days; you're going to feel better. Maybe you like to have candy or chocolate before you go to bed. Say, "You know what I'm not going to eat two hours before bed." You stick to that for 21 days and it becomes a lot easier.

Sure, you can have that habit. I had habits years and years ago that I still think about. Occasionally I get in a situation that could trigger one of those bad habits, but I don't let it. I take control; there's no reason to go back. You know what usually works is you have to set a date. You say, "Okay, I'm going to start today and do whatever it is for the next 21 days." Put it on your calendar or in your journal, write it down somewhere, make notes, or put it in your phone and set an alarm. In 21 days that alarm goes off and shows you've just accomplished what you wanted to for the last 21 days. Then you put in the date for 90 days and you strive for that goal.

If you fail to reach that goal, start over with the experience you gained, and try again. Going back to square one and starting over takes extreme willpower, courage and strength. You have everything you need with inside of you.

Once you reach that milestone it becomes a lifestyle. Good or bad, whatever you wanted to change is now part of your lifestyle; the neurons in your brain that were firing and leading to the wrong thing that you wanted to stop are now firing in a way that makes you think differently about whatever change you've made. The 21-90 rule is a helpful tool to help you make the changes in your life you wish to make.

Think about it. You take three weeks to make a change. It's not even a whole month. It's just three weeks out of your life to change something about yourself that you've wanted to address. Maybe you don't smoke for three weeks, but it can be anything in life that you want to change. Do it for three weeks, and when you get through that period, <u>the habit has been broken.</u> Then maintain the change for three months to make it a lifestyle. You can do it. It's a self-timed goal, it's a challenge that you impose upon yourself and you do it to get stronger.

You have to really push to achieve these goals in your life to actually become what you want to become.

You have to understand the why. What is your why? Why do you want to change something about yourself? If you want to lose weight, is it for you so you feel better, or is it to feel more attractive to other people, or to attract somebody? If you're doing it for someone other than yourself, then the energy of the Why is not going to be strong enough to help you achieve that goal. The Why has to be something coming from deep inside your soul. In order for you to stick to your goal of doing or not doing something for 21 days, you have to understand the why.

Okay, it's not going to be easy. Trust me…this is not going to be easy because your subconscious mind has been so trained to feel a certain way because you've done a certain thing and now you don't want to do that thing. So, at first it's going to feel very uncomfortable. It's going to feel totally uncomfortable and, you're not going to want to do it. A voice in your head is going to say, Forget it. We can't do this. Let's give up. Let's go back to the other way that I feel comfortable. That lifestyle we've had for all these years that we haven't changed. Your subconscious is telling you we're used to that old comfortable way. We don't want to feel uncomfortable.

As soon as you start feeling uncomfortable, just remind yourself that you are making a change. If your brain and your body are saying, "Hey, what are you doing, we're feeling uncomfortable?" Then you know you're doing something right…that you are actually on the right track. I know that and believe it. Don't fall into that other trap. As soon as you believe it, and you understand the why you will want to change it.

Don't fall into the trap of negative self-talk either. Let's say you want to lose weight or you want to exercise. Then just say, "Well, I've never been one to exercise, but I'll try it." Next you have to change your personal reality. Change the way you think about yourself in order to change yourself. Does that make sense? I hope it does, because the only way you're going to change is to change the way you visualize yourself, the way you think about yourself, your self-talk…all of your self-talk. Listen to me or whoever is motivating you to give you the strength and willpower and the self-talk and the self-confidence to do the things in life that you really want to do.

Then by all means, I hope I am one of the reasons that you've made the change in your life, but it really wasn't me. Just know that it was you. I only helped you open the doors to your mind and helped you realize your capability. YOU can do anything. So if you want to change your life try the 21-90 rule.

I've actually done it in the past because I've made some major changes, but I just didn't have a name for the rule. I just did something over and over for a long period of time; it changed my lifestyle and changed my life. But you need to put a time limit on it and actually have a goal to reach, then this is the plan for you. The 21-90 rule. Use it for anything you want to change. Just go 21 days and break the bad habit or start a new good one, and then continue 90 days to make it a lasting part of your lifestyle. Three months and it becomes a part of your lifestyle and your life will change for the better. Trust me you will have the self-confidence to do anything you want… anything! And just know, just know that you can do whatever you put your mind too.

Think about it…you can do it. You can do it! Let's make the change in our life. Let's be better. Let's be better people.

Chapter 9

What If You Knew Your Future?

Think about that for a second. What would you do if you knew you were the creator of your destiny? Would you ever miss a day? Would you be more confident and make better decisions?

But the fact of the matter is you are creating your life. If you want to change your life because you're not happy with it you must begin to think about what you've been thinking about. If you don't like where you are then you have to change your thoughts.

It's very important to know what you're thinking about because you're actually creating your future. You are creating your destiny. You are literally in total control of the emotions that anchor you to your past. In order to change your way of thinking and change your personality, you must change your personal reality. You literally must become someone else. You can't create a new personal reality with the same personality. You can't become someone else if you're still trying to be the same person. If you want your life to be different, you have to change your way of thinking.

When you're constantly living in the past, remembering things from the past, creating those emotional links in your mind and feeling the past you're not going to get away from it. You

~ The Positive Perspective ~

continue to produce the same outcome because you are not becoming conscious of your thoughts. Simply becoming aware of your thoughts is huge. Once you are aware of what you are thinking and what those thoughts are creating, you can begin to change them. That's when you begin to create new habits.

"Insanity is doing the same thing over and over and expecting a different outcome."

If you're don't do anything different, your life is not going to change. You're going to be stuck in the program of the past. You can say I'm going to be positive or I'm going to change my life. I'm going to get a better job and get a better house. But then you don't change anything about yourself, you just think about it sometimes but aren't really doing anything to change it.

But be prepared! When you try to do something that's different from your past it's going to feel uncomfortable your body doesn't like it. Why? Because for many years it's been programmed to do a certain thing and to run that program over and over again. So when you do something out of the ordinary it's uncomfortable.

So begin by saying to yourself, I am smart, I am pretty I am the weight I want to be. When you say I am your commanding your mind towards your destiny. OK. When you say I am. you are committing it to your mind and you're making starting to make that change if you're not filling your mind with visions of your future you're left with the old habits of your past.

Let me say that one more time:

If you are not filling your mind with the visions of the future, you're left with the old habits of your past.

Okay. Now I have a question for you. It's about belief. Now a lot of people have faith in God. A lot of people have belief in things. Can you believe in a future that you can't see if you can't actually see the future? Can you actually believe it?

You can if you visualize it enough your mind. If you visualize your future enough in your mind you can trick your mind into thinking it's the actual future because your mind does not know the difference between imagination and reality. It's been proven science says that you can change your future just by thinking. You begin to plan your behaviors you get closer to who you want to be. That mental rehearsal actually installs the circuits in your brain which makes your brain a map to the future not a record of the past.

Right now your brain is a record of your past.

You wake up in the morning and you think about the problems that you had you think about your bills you think about work. You think about things that have already happened and you predict what's going to happen. That's why when you wake up sometimes you're like oh I don't want to do this today because you're actually thinking about what your habit has been created. All this time and what your subconscious mind thinks is going to happen. It's predicting the future which it cannot do. It's living out what you've trained it to do.

It's running the program. Your brain is a computer. It's running the program that it's been taught for so many years and it's very hard to change a program in your brain without rewiring your thoughts. You must break the thoughts of your past and your old habits and create new ones. So when you are visualizing your future in your mind and you're doing it over and over again, you're living it. You can experience it with all your emotion.

When this happens you are no longer waiting for happiness or success because in your mind you've already experienced it. It's so much easier for it to come into reality because you've already experienced the feeling of success before it happened. So when it comes to you it's no surprise.

But the more you do it the more it's like the game it's like oh I could just manifest my life. I can actually create my destiny. If you knew you could create your destiny wouldn't you do that every day? Your mind cannot distinguish between imagination and reality. It's a scientific fact. I think there was a test with some basketball players where they had half the team actually practice all week and the other half a team just go in isolation and visualize practicing and they tested brainwaves and muscle response and they were almost exactly the same. The ones that were just visualizing, the muscles were actually firing the way they would if you they actually playing. You see your brain doesn't know the difference.

So in order to retrain your brain you have to unlearn your past habits and create your new self. You just have to have those new thoughts to create your new self. When most people get up in the morning they think about their problems. Those

~ The Positive Perspective ~

problems are circuits in the brain representing past experiences. Each one of these circuits are connected to people, places, emotions, and feelings from the past. So as soon as you get up and you start thinking about all that stuff you're starting your day off. In the past so when you recall those experiences of the past emotions come along with it how you think how you feel create your state of being.

So when you think about the past you start your day off in the past. The more you do this the more it becomes your predictable future. You will be creating the same life because you're repeatedly thinking about the past and not thinking about the future. So you actually have no control over your life because you're not disconnecting from those old thoughts and creating new thoughts and new dreams. Every day you go through repeating the same things driving the same way interacting with the same people that becomes your program. You're like a hamster in a wheel going through the same thing over and over again and in order to change your life.

You have to change your thoughts. So the fact is you do create your destiny. You can create your destiny every single day so you should know that your future is 100 percent in your hands because you are the creator of your destiny.

Your thoughts create your life what you think about you bring about. You have to remember that. Your life and where you are right now is a product of your past thoughts.

So if you keep thinking in the past you're going to stay right where you are and you're not going to get to that next plateau of happiness. And that's what we're trying to do we're trying to

~ The Positive Perspective ~

get happy right. I want to be happy don't you? You can create your destiny so do it.

Be happy
     Think positive.
          Create happy thoughts.

Chapter 10

Leaving Your Comfort Zone Behind

We all have our comfort zone. The place where feelings are very predictable. But sometimes you can get too comfortable in your comfort zone and you start feeling uncomfortable. Have you ever felt that? I know I have. When you feel like you're just going through the motions or going along for the ride, you're really not in control of your life. You're just not taking any risks. You're not doing anything and your life isn't getting any better. It becomes so predictable and mundane that it's not enjoyable anymore. You're afraid to venture out. You're afraid to get out of that comfort zone. There's no thrill in your life. There's nothing new.

When you realize it you may get a little nervous that your life is never going to change. You stop trying to advance you life, your relationship or your job. You have accepted that you're never going to get anything better.

So how do you get out of that comfort zone and still feel safe enough to go on with your life and to take some risk? Well, you must to step out of your comfort zone. You just have to do it. What if you never do it? What's the harm in not stepping out of your comfort zone? What's the worst thing that can happen? Well, you know, it the worst thing that could happen is regret.

If you never take any chances and you never try anything new and you go through your whole life flatlining. You're never going to experience life to the fullest and probably won't get to enjoy all life has to offer. It would be a shame to miss out on so much in life because you refuse to take any chances or to do anything different. So think about that for a minute. Is it time to step out of your comfort zone?

There is something better out there for you if you just step into that river of change.

Stop listening to people that say, "play it safe. Just do the predictable thing and you'll be OK. Don't take too many chances". Those are probably the same people that aren't taking any chances and are probably not getting any further in life. They're happy doing the same job, doing the same things, going to the same places, wearing the same clothes and not moving forward.

How boring is that? That's not what life is. Life is not meant to be sitting around doing the same thing over and over again. We're here on this planet to experience life, to enjoy life, to live it to the fullest and to experience new things. Be of aware the people that are trying to hold you back, they are afraid of change too.

Don't be afraid. Don't let their fear rub off on you. If you are starting to feel uncomfortable in your comfort zone, that is a good thing. Why? Because that means you are becoming aware of your true potential. You are realizing that your mind is in control of your life. Your thoughts are creating your future.

Once you do, be warned, you're going to feel uncomfortable as hell. When you start doing something different in your life, your body does not like it. It wants what it knows. When it's uncomfortable, your body will try to tell your brain to go back to the old way. It does not want to experiment with the unknown. This is where your thirst for change, your desire for something new or better must take over. Use these thoughts to energize your willpower so you can move forward.

You control your mind and your mind controls your body.

More happiness will come, more fulfilling things will come to you when you start taking chances and stepping out of that comfort zone. Don't pay attention to the people that are trying to hold you back because they're too afraid themselves. They're angry with themselves, because they're too afraid to do the things that they really want to do. They will be the ones experiencing regret in their life.

You may be thinking I'm going to ask for a raise or I'm going to ask this person out on a date or I am going to try skydiving or you want to start a business. Whatever it is, DO IT! You have to do it. You have to go for it. Because there is nothing worse than living in regret. Going through your life, playing it safe, living in the comfort zone, not following your dreams always leads to regret.

When you get to the end of your life and you can't do all these things that you've thought about, you're going to think what if what if I would have asked that person to marry me? What if I would have taken that vacation or if I would have gone parasailing or bungee jumping or hang gliding? Just do it because it will add excitement to your life. Don't worry about the people that are going to condemn you for it and try to talk you out of it. Take a look at their life. What are they doing? What are they experiencing? How happy are they? What's missing from their life? Are they just doing the same thing over and over? Because it's secure, because it's predictable, because it's what their parents did. It doesn't matter. What do you want to do with your life? OK. So when your comfort zone starts getting uncomfortable, go ahead and explore. Do some research. Figure out something else that you want to do that's different from the normal thing that you do every single day and the rut that you've gotten yourself into a boring, mundane life. Change it. Make your life exciting.

Nobody's going to knock on the door and say here's your exciting life. I've got something really exciting for you. You have to do it for yourself. You have to take control of your life and step into that river of uncertainty. Don't be afraid of the unknown and try something new. It will be uncomfortable. You're not gonna like it at first because it's not predictable, you're not used to it and you don't have the immediate answers. You will have to search for the answers. You will find solutions and explore opportunities and your life will blossom. Trust me, it will. But if you stay in that comfort zone, if you live the life of predictability, you're going to have exactly that, a boring life. Who wants that? I don't want that. You don't want that. So let's get excited and get out of the comfort zone. Especially if you're feeling uncomfortable in it.

Creating that fear in your mind will create a scenario that is way worse in the worst case scenario. When you fail and you get up and you try again and you learn.

Remember, Failure is not a bad thing.

So repeat this to your self at least once a day. *I've got enough energy, confidence and desire to create my full happy life. I will step out of my comfort zone. I am not afraid to try new things. My mind controls my body.*

I like a challenge, and I'm hoping that you do, too. So step out of your comfort zone. Be happy, experience life to the fullest and really enjoy this gift of life that we've been given. You're not gonna be here forever. Don't live in the sea of regret.

Chapter 11

How Important Are Material Things?

I've got a question for you. Do material things even matter? The quantity of stuff that you have doesn't really matter. Does it change your life? Well, it could. If you've got a nice fancy car you've got a really big house. It does change the quality of your life but does it really change how you feel about your life? Now what do I mean by that? You can have a lot of stuff and all kinds of things and be unhappy. There are a lot of people who have a lot of things that aren't even happy and that's terrible.

You can attract all these things into your life and get this a lot of money and get the nice house and the cars and take all the trips and it sounds like a glamorous lifestyle. But if you're not happy with yourself, if you don't like the inner person that you are then all of that stuff is meaningless. Having all the things you want really doesn't matter if you're not happy and that's the bottom line.

My whole purpose writing this book and doing my positive podcast is to help you to be happy. I want to help you to be positive and help you to find that inner happiness and live your life with total happiness and positivity. When you project happiness and get on the wavelength of positivity, all that positivity and happiness will come back to you. Then you can actually enjoy your life and isn't that what we all want?

You can enjoy your life just by choosing to.

You choose how you respond to any situation. You can react to it or you can respond to it. You choose how you feel because you have control over only one thing, your thoughts. So what am I even talking about here? I'm talking about material things and do they have any bearing on your happiness? They can be a reward for your happiness. Go with me on this. You plan your life. You think about what you're thinking about. You focus on your goals and you work towards your goals you start achieving your goals.

Maybe it's financial goals, maybe you want ten thousand dollars in the bank by the end of the year. Maybe success to you is having all those material things like expensive cars, watches, houses , etc. Maybe that is how you show everyone else that you're successful. But if you are not truly happy inside, none of those things matter because our purpose in life is to be happy.

How do you define success?

Some people have a loving family, a decent job making average money, they have a roof over their head, they have food in their fridge and they have clothes on their back. They smile every day and they're happy, <u>really happy</u>. They're not filthy rich but they have enough to get them by and they are content. To them that is the definition of success and that is perfectly fine.

Success is whatever you say it is.

It's not what the world says success is. What other people think doesn't matter it's what you think that counts. Because if you're not happy inside all the *stuff* in the world is not going to make you a happy person. But if you are content and happy, you do the right things, think positively and put out that positive energy and you decide to reward yourself with luxurious things, that's fine. You worked hard in your life, you deserve it. You have to work at it and always be in control of your thoughts.

Now society has really changed the way they think about material things. We live in a disposable society. A lot of people think that they can just throw things away instead of repairing them. They can just get a new one or they don't take care what they have because they have the money to buy a new one. In this day and age you have to appreciate what you have.

Wake up every morning and be thankful for what you have whether it's hardly anything or whether it is an abundance of things. You must express gratitude, be thankful and say out loud, thank you, thank you, thank you for everything that I have.

I literally say it 3 times every morning. I am truly grateful to wake up everyday!

Whether it's a crappy job that barely pays the bills but keeps food on the table or it's a million dollar a year job that lets you fly around the world in a jet, you must be thankful for what you have and show gratitude every day.

I don't really care a lot about material things. I have some but I have what I need. I'd like to have more but that is not the most important thing to me. Family, happiness, giving back, paying it forward and sharing positivity, that's what is important to me. Leaving a good impression on this planet is very important to me.

I want people to say wow that guy really helped me out a lot. I learned how to be happy. He was really positive and happy all the time.

Chapter 12

Your Inner Voice Doesn't Lie

Get To Know Your Inner Voice. How do I stay positive and keep negativity out of my thoughts? One word, gratitude. It's that simple. I am grateful for all that I have. I'm happy to be alive everyday. When I wake up I'm thankful that I actually got to wake up again. I listen to my positive inner voice, the voice that does not care what people think or say. Make sure your inner voice is voicing positivity. If your inner voice is constantly feeding you negative thoughts, start there. Start by thinking positive thoughts. Think about the good that can come out of situations not the "worst case scenario". Create the new habit of optimism and positivity. Teach your negative inner voice how to be positive.

I'm happy to be who I am and the things in my life that I don't like I change. You can't change the past but you can actually manipulate your thoughts to create your future which is what I'm doing right now. I am creating my future, moment by moment with the thoughts and pictures hold in my mind. I don't let negativity in. I try not to let things bother me like they used to. I think of how to be positive and how to benefit my life and others around me.

People that are relentlessly trying to make you feel bad or negative, will eventually give up as long as you don't let them to put that negativity on you. Simply do not accept it. It's no fun for them because it's not working on you. It's fun for you because you're actually perpetuating the happiness and they don't know what to do with themselves.

I do it all the time and it's great. I end up making other people happy and making other people's day. It's so rewarding to actually put a smile on somebody's face whether it's to buy them lunch or by giving them a compliment. When you pay someone a compliment, say good morning or just ask them how is your day and then actually listen to what they have to say about their day, you'd be surprised how good it makes them feel. Don't forget other people are important too.

Why are other people important when you need to focus on yourself and your life? Every single person is important. You know why? Because we're all the same. We all come from the same energy. We're basically all the same thing just in different physical bodies. We are a physical manifestation of our spiritual energy.

Now there's some kind of quantum physics that says all things are created from the same energy and we will all end up in the same place. It's a whole big schpiel that I'm not going to get into. I'm not a science major. All I know is I can feel things from other people when I'm talking to them. I feel energies coming from other people when I pay attention to their energy. If you pay attention to a persons body language or look into their eyes you will feel something. There will be a connection, good or bad, there will be a connection. Have you ever met someone for the first time and you just didn't get along? You didn't know why, you just had a gut feeling that you couldn't shake. That is your mind picking up on their energy and their thoughts. Have you ever walked into a room and just didn't feel right? If you just pay attention to how people talk and how someone is reacting to your conversation you can tell a lot about that person.

Don't argue with your inner voice!

Nothing will change unless you do. You must take pride in yourself, grab that willpower and decide for yourself, I'm going to change. I'm going to change the way I am. You may have thoughts like, I'm not going to eat so much. I'm going to lose weight. I'm going to exercise. I'm going to do better at my job. I'm going to treat my spouse better I'm going to treat myself better. I'm going to pursue my idea. I'm going to whatever it is that you're not doing. Hopefully you're getting motivated to do it. Just thinking about things that you want to do and saying oh I could do this I could do that is not enough. You must become the mind. You must tell your body, "you will do as I say". Above all you gotta mean it.

Most people don't get past the thought of it. They don't pursue it and don't hold the thought of their success and their dreams in their minds and think about it everyday.

When the going gets tough it's going to get hard. There's going to be times when you fall on your face, when you're going to fail at something.

Don't focus on the failure, focus on the lesson learned.

Don't look at it as like it's over. It's not a failure. It's just one more way that doesn't work. That is now out of your way. You see, you can turn anything around to be a positive for you.

So you try something and fail. Say to yourself, well that didn't work. So now I know that doesn't work, let me try a different approach. Maybe it will work, maybe it won't but you keep trying different strategies until you figure it out. Never give up, eventually you will crack the code and you will get through. You will be successful. You will get what you want if you are relentless in the pursuit of your desire.

You must be relentless in creating the good habits, doing the positive things and keep the positive thoughts in your mind. Even one negative thought in your mind can temporarily derail your positivity. Negativity will find its way into your mind with no problem. It doesn't need any help it just comes right in. It's how you respond to the negativity that determines your positive mindset. You have to plant the seeds of positivity in your mind in order to reach your goals and dreams.

My goal with this book is to help you find your happiness, to learn how to love yourself and love others, and to learn how to be strong. Be strong enough to fail, get up try it again and fail. Failure is not the end, it is the beginnings of success. Every successful person has failed. The difference is they did not give up. They got back up, brushed themselves off, came up with a new plan and tried again and again until they succeeded. Their positive inner voice guided them.

Whether it's moving out of your house, standing on your own two feet financially, asking that person on a date, or buying that new car listen to what your heart is telling you. If you listen, you'll know what will really make you happy. Act on that feeling because this part of your journey will come to an end. Your life is not that long when you think about it. Pretty soon it's gonna be over and you're going to say I wish I would have done this I wish I would have done that. I wish I would have taken that trip. I wish I would have asked that girl to dance. Remember regret is a terrible feeling. If you wait until the time is right you'll never do anything because the time will never be right. The saddest thing to see is the regret in a persons eyes when he realizes he can no longer pursue his dream because it is too late.

You have to follow through with your ideas or you're never going to know if you might have reached your goal.

~ The Positive Perspective ~

Chapter 13

Teaching Positivity To Your Children

The idea for this chapter came to me while I was talking with my daughter. I wondered, am I teaching her positivity? There are so many people that aren't taking the time to teach children that their mind controls their body. They're not raising their children to be positive. They are planting self imposed limitations in their child's subconscious mind that will follow them throughout their life. How do you teach your kids positivity and give them self-confidence? Is it important to teach them that they can be all they want to be as long as they truly believe they can? How do you teach them that their mindset determines their reality?

The best way is to lead by example. You have to live that way yourself. You can't be disorganized or an untrusting or a person who doesn't believe in a higher power and expect your children to be organized or trusting.

As they grow up they will have their own thoughts and have their own perspective on life and do their own thing. But in the beginning, when they're younger you have the opportunity to train their mind. You have to load up their subconscious with positivity and give them the tools to succeed.

When they're babies you have to be careful what you expose them to. Be aware of what thoughts you are introducing to their subconscious. Children are like sponges. They absorb and retain almost everything you say. If you fill their minds with negativity and continually speak negatively or constantly speak of lack, they will grow up thinking there is not enough in the world for them. The universe is infinite so there is enough of everything for everyone.

Teach them they can have, be or do whatever they can think of. Always let tell them they can fulfill their dreams by being positive and having a plan. As they get older and become teenagers then adults, keep reinforcing positivity. Listen to them and believe in their dreams, support them no matter what. Even when they seem to be changing too fast for you. Let them become who they are. Let them create.

When they become teenagers it's hard to actually instill the positivity in them because they are trying to be independent. Reinforce to them that what they think about, they bring about. How they project themselves is how other people will see them and what their future will bring them is totally within their control.If you have a negative outlook on life and you believe the world is cruel and miserable and everyone is out to get you, your children will pick up on that and they will begin to feel the same way.

Children need guidance, they need praise as well as discipline. If they expect negativity, that's what they're going to experience. If you are emitting negativity, that's what their energy is going to be. On the other hand if they believe that their life is full of joy and happiness the universe will support them and the infinite intelligence will put circumstances and events in motion to help them achieve them they will prosper.

It's so critical to help them develop an attitude of gratitude. Being thankful for what you have, taking care of what you have and appreciating everything that is good in your life. Did you know when you appreciate everything that's good in your life, more good things will come to you? What you think about you bring about.

The energy you put out there is the same energy that you get back.

So when you're trying to teach your children to be positive and they get in this slump to where they just don't care or they're just going through life and not actually controlling themselves it's your opportunity to teach them that they have the mind power to accomplish anything. Teach them to become aware of what they are thinking.

Habits, good or bad, are very hard to break. With willpower and repetition new habits can be created. It's your job as a parent to teach them and help them to learn good habits. That's not going to be easy at first and they're not going to understand it. It is your job to explain to them that the habits they have now are the habits that will be with them their entire life. Habits are a reflection of who we really are. They affect their life in many ways. The person they are, the job they have, the people the meet, the person they fall in love with, the house they'll have the car they'll drive the money they'll acquire. As the parent, you have to help them learn to be focused and positive. To actually take control their mind.

Here's a few simple ways to teach your child good habits.

1. Have them make their bed. The simple act of making your bed first thing in the morning creates a sense of accomplishment to start your day. It's a positive reinforcement that starts your day off right. A task completed.

2. Keeping their room clean. The simple act of keeping their room clean as opposed to cleaning it up once a month teaches them discipline. By keeping their room clean instead of just cleaning it up they will learn the value of being and staying organized.

3. Making sure they do their homework. Doing homework is something required but not always enjoyed. There's things in life we all must do that we would rather not do. However, life doesn't always work that way. It's like having a job. You need to work to pay bills. Procrastinating only prolongs the unpleasantness.

4. Respect. This habit is so important to success it should be first on this list. Respect is not being taught to our children. Respecting their elders, authority and their parents. You can't just say well they're just teenagers we'll just let it go. You will be a failure as a parent if you let your children just grow up on their own.

It's your job to teach them right. When you teach your children to focus on the good things and positivity, more good things will come to them. You can reward them when they clean their room or they do their homework. You can reward them with ice cream or they can stay up later. If you want to use money you can use money but do whatever it takes to teach them the good habits, they deserve it and it's worth it.

Neuroscientists have long studied the benefits of practicing the attitude of gratitude and they discovered it literally changes the molecular structure of your brain and makes you a happier healthier person.

Be grateful for all that you have. It's not enough that you feel appreciative but you must to be grateful, really grateful. Teach your kids gratitude and it will help them to be positive. Make them be thankful for what they have. It's so important to raise your children positively and to teach them things that will make them better people in life. It's your job as a parent to raise your children and to raise positive kids.

Don't let them be messy. Don't let them talk back to you. Don't let them be rude. Don't let them take advantage of a situation. Don't let them rule the house. Don't let them run the family. Remember, you're the parent. You run the show, raise your children so they become great adults.

Chapter 14

Staying Positive With Willpower

Having the will power to stay positive and take control of your mind is paramount. If you've made mistakes in your past and you think that it's affecting your future, I'm here to tell you you're wrong. Why do I say that with such conviction? Because what you did in your past is just that, it's your past and your past does not dictate your future, unless you let it. Your future depends on the decisions you make, the actions you take, and the thoughts you think. In every moment of your life you are creating your future with your thoughts. Think about that for a while. Everything you do, everything you think everything and you say is creating your future. Your past has created your present. What you've done in your past has brought you to this point. Your future is created by the actions and the thoughts you think most. Having the will power to be persistent and becoming aware of your thoughts will feed your subconscious mind the positivity it needs.

If you don't like where you are in life, change your thoughts. Change the pictures in your mind; change the way you think and your life will change. You must change who you are. Change your personality to change you personal reality. You are who you are because of the decisions you've made. If you keep doing the same thing and thinking the same thoughts you're going to end up in the same place a year from now, 10 years from now, 20 years from now.

Nothing will change unless you do. You have to change your thoughts to change your life. In order to do that, you must create new habits and become aware of your thoughts. You will need to step into that river of change.

Be aware, when you step into that river of change, it will feel very uncomfortable. Your body will not like it at first. Your subconscious mind will try to talk you out of it because it wants to go back to the comfortable feeling of habit. It will say things like you can't do that, or that's not what we're used to. This isn't you. You'll never change. This is when your willpower becomes very important.

Once you become aware of your thoughts and you get through the "river of change," it gets easier and easier. You start to create NEW habits — positive, healthy habits that start to bring you happiness.

There are people that are always happy and I mean really happy. Not just on the outside either. Happy people are happy because they practice. They have the willpower to do whatever it takes to be happy. They've learned habits that make them happy. They don't let the outside world affect their feeling. Sure, they've made mistakes in their past but they're not letting past mistakes dictate their future. They do not hold on to the past. They learn from the mistakes, they move on and they continue to move forward.

~ The Positive Perspective ~

I think the saying is, the definition of insanity is doing the same thing over and over again and expecting a different outcome? So if you're doing the same thing that you've done for the past ten, twenty, thirty plus years, and you are expecting a change, I've got some bad news, it ain't gonna change!

Your life is not going to get better unless you change your thoughts. You must literally change the way you think, the way you act and the way you feel. Start appreciating your life and this gift that you've been given. You really have to appreciate yourself and be proud of yourself. Stay positive about the things in your life even when bad things happen. The old saying, when something bad happens something good always comes out of it. If you look hard enough, you'll find it. If you can't find it, create it. Turn the negative into positive. Find that *Positive Perspective.*

Imagine you're driving from Florida to California at night. You can only see about a hundred feet in front of you with the headlights but you know California is at the end of your road. You know if you look for the next hundred feet and you follow those lights, you'll eventually get to your destination. Well, your life is like that too. You can't predict your future for the next thirty years you have to just take it one step at a time. You must constantly be moving forward into your future while creating your present with the thoughts in your mind.

Your thoughts are very powerful. They are the creators of your life. Staying positive and remaining focused are the keys to your happiness along with having the will power to do so. Don't dwell on your past because you can't change it. (I'm intentionally putting this sentence in the book twice so you get it.) Don't dwell on your past because you can't change it. The only thing you have absolute control over are your thoughts. Your past does not dictate your future because the thoughts you are thinking right now are creating your future. The pictures in your mind combined with your energy, be it positive or negative, will attract the persistent thoughts in your mind to you.

I think everyone really wants to be a nice person but some blame their past for their negative actions or their situation. They think that it is a good enough excuse. It is not! Being negative, being a bad person, doing illegal things or being self-destructive is not helping. You know it isn't right deep in your gut. "It's because of my past, it's because I had mean parents". Placing blame outside of yourself for any situation is just a cop-out because you, and only you have control of your mind.

When you blame an outside source you are admitting that you are not in control of your life. You are admitting that you don't have the desire to control your own destiny. When you become aware of this you can take the power back. You will realize that you are in control of your body and you are in total control of your destiny. Your past cannot dictate your future and I can't say that enough.

It's hard to understand this concept if you've been blaming your past for a log time. That's okay because you're reading this book and now you can begin to make the changes you've been thinking about but have yet to act upon. It's time to accept the fact that the decisions you have made in your life have gotten you to where you are today, but you don't have to stay there. You can make the change by changing your way of

~ The Positive Perspective ~

thinking. You're the only person that is in charge of your life. You have the capabilities to control your mind and change the way you think about any situation. Always remember to think about what you're thinking about and make sure there are only positive thoughts in your mind.

Be energetic in your life. Life was made to be abundant, energetic and fun. If you're not happy and enjoying your life it's a crying shame. I wish I could just come to your house and show you how to be happy but I can't do that. Hopefully my words will give you the tools you need and convince you that you have the power to manifest anything you desire in life. Be it happiness, wealth, material things, anything you desire. You have the power inside of you to make the changes that you want to make, to live a better life. Only you have the power to push those negative thoughts out and fill your mind with positivity and positive thoughts. But it takes will power, it takes a burning desire, it takes persistence and determination. It also takes 100% belief that you can achieve whatever it is you desire.

If you don't like the situation you're in and you aren't ready get out of it right away, keep visualizing the new situation. Visualize where you want to be and your life will change. Feel the feelings you will feel when you reach that destination, when you accomplish that goal. Feel it! You'll start attracting positivity. You will emit positive energy that will only attract the same. You'll begin finding ways to be happier and that's what this is all about.

This is all about helping you to find your way to be happy. It's not about me telling you how to be happy. It's about opening up your mind and learning how you can control your own happiness. Once you get control of that and understand it, you won't need me anymore because you'll be a happy person, and I'm fine with that.

The goal is for you to control your mind, control your happiness and practice happy positive thoughts. As soon as you notice a negative thought, address it and release it. If you dwell on it, it's going to drag you down and it's going to keep you from that happy future that you deserve. You can really do whatever you want to do so why not think about creating a better future for yourself through your positive thoughts now?

Many of us wait until a crisis to decide to make a change, my question is why wait? Why wait until you get diagnosed with lung cancer before you quit smoking? Why wait until you get diabetes before you regulate your sugar intake? Why wait until you hate your job so much it literally makes sick before you look for a new one? Why stay in a destructive relationship before you get out of it? Why wait until you're so overweight you can't tie your shoes without getting out of breath?

Wouldn't be much easier to make changes in your life under happy, less stressful situations?

All of these things are your choice, everything you do is by your choice and the sooner you accept that, the easier it will be to move forward. Remember, thoughts become things.

Chapter 15

Dealing With Medical Issues?

Doctors and hospitals are scary am I right? We all have to go to the doctor and the fear feels real. But what happens to you after you get a negative diagnosis from the doctor? How do you cope with the doctor telling you you've got a chronic illness that's going to last you for the rest of your life and it's going to change the way you live? How do you cope with a loved one that is being diagnosed with that and that you have to deal with?

There are so many sides to this. When something with our health goes south we feel helpless. What most people don't realize is that we can heal ourselves. I believe that the mind controls the body and the mind can heal the body. The human body can produce any pharmaceutical cure it needs if you expand your consciousness.

If you have been diagnosed with a disease that is going to change your life maybe a chronic illness that could last for a year or last your lifetime. It really changes your lifestyle. Let's say you have to have chemotherapy or you have to do a drug regimen or you have to live with someone who is going through it. It can cause a drastic change in your lifestyle.

~ The Positive Perspective ~

The emotional stress can often be overwhelming. The self blame starts with thoughts like why did this happen to me? You begin to feel sorry for yourself. The depression can kick in. Everyone reacts differently but I can tell you this, how respond to any negativity determines how your life will play out.

My family and I have been blessed with health. So I'm not speaking from personal experience I am just speaking from what I see. If you have found out that you have a terminal illness and you know you're not going to survive, guess what? None of us are going to survive. The only way out of this life is death. Think about it, everybody is going to die. Just finding out and knowing that you're going to when someone else tells you is devastating. If you don't know, then you still go on with your life as normal. It's when you find out that you change your life. You shouldn't change the person you are because of a diagnosis like that. I know it might sound easy to say, but I think that if I was diagnosed with something terminal, (after the devastation set in and I accepted my fate) I would deal with it and I would turn it to a positive spin and try to share energy through my illness.

Maybe you choose not to tell anybody in your family that you're ill and just go on with your life and slowly fade away. Maybe that's what you want to do. And you know what? It's OK. It's your life, and your death. You choose how you want to deal with it. But you have to also keep your positivity, accept your fate and move on. It's easy to say, but you could get really depressed knowing that you're going to die. Guess what? If you get diagnosed with a perfect bill of health and you think about dying, you're gonna get depressed. I think it's the knowing and having a clock ticking in your mind that can be very depressing. Every one of us has a ticking clock — we just don't know how long we have.

Be connected to your body, become aware of what's going on in your body and make changes in your diet, in your in your thoughts and live a healthier lifestyle. The best way to cope with the negative medical diagnosis, whether it's on you or someone you love, is to actually accept it. Accept that it's happening. You can't go back in a time machine and change the past.

If you don't accept it, you can't move on to the next phase. You can't enjoy the rest of your life. You can't really do anything or get better. It's now part of life, a part of your life. It's the cards you're dealt. So you have to move on. Don't be afraid to reach out to your higher power, to the infinite intelligence, to God, whoever you think is the superior being in your world, reach out to them and get guidance and talk into in your mind with the spirit world and you will find answers, you will be happier and be grateful for every day.

I say it every day when I wake up. I am so thankful and so grateful that I got to wake up again.

If you were diagnosed with a chronic illness or a terminal illness that becomes even more prevalent in your life, you should feel happy that you got to wake up again. You actually are alive and can contribute to society and live a happy fulfilling life. Show gratitude every day.

Having a chronic illness doesn't mean that your life is over. There's people that have lost all their limbs or that they've gone blind or whatever, or they've got cancer and they do great things. It's all in how you choose to accept it. So challenge yourself to find your strengths in the in this whole thing that happens.

Experience joy even when you're in pain. Find the silver lining. Dealing with a chronic illness is no walk in the park. It can be challenging. It can totally devastate you. It can ruin your life if you let it. But don't. Look ahead. You have to take it day by day. You accept what happens, accept the things you can't change and be positive and be happy.

Every one of us is going to die some sooner than others. Some are going to live forever like Keith Richards. So don't worry about it. It's inevitable for everyone. You can't get out alive. So enjoy every day you have whether you know the end is near or not. Leave a positive mark on this planet that you are proud of. Be an inspiration to people. Give people hope. Give them strength through your actions, your feelings and your positive motivation.

You can share the positivity even in a negative situation. When you learn to do that, you have made a mark on the world.

Be happy that you've got another day. Wake up in the morning and be grateful. Be thankful and show it in everything you do.

~ The Positive Perspective ~

Chapter 16

Negative Thoughts Ruin Your Life?

Why do you think people fail while trying to achieve their goals? It's not the lack of money. It's not the absence of time. It's not bad luck. The biggest reason why so many people struggle to achieve exactly what they want in their life is because they let their mind take them out of the game. More specifically they let their beliefs and their thoughts stop them from taking action.

That's right your beliefs and your thoughts will trap you and keep you doing the same thing over and over again expecting different results. It's easy to get stuck in your comfort zone and never make any progress.

Let me begin by saying your mind is really controlling everything including your present, your past and your future. You are creating your life with your mind, with every single thought you have. Some people will not get to the highest level of success because they're going to continue to live in the past. They're not going to take the risks needed to succeed. They continue to put themselves down and not believe in themselves. Because of these thoughts and emotions they will not accomplish the things they want to accomplish because they're afraid to take the risk. So in reality, they're afraid to actually think for themselves.

If you want to succeed at you highest level, you're going to have to be aware of your thoughts. You are going to need to have a burning desire so you can manifest the willpower to follow through with your goals. One of the affirmations I always say is ***think about what you're thinking about.*** If you're not controlling your thoughts and intentionally creating your thoughts, you're just letting life happen to you and you are not in control. When that happens, you're really not thinking about what you're thinking about, your mind is just like the wild west and your life is running awry. You don't have control over it because you have not learned to control it.

I know it sounds strange but your thoughts are responsible for your actions. Your thoughts are responsible for your past; they are creating your present and are the road to your future. Your thoughts create your life and you are responsible for creating your thoughts. If you aren't aware of what you're thinking about, your thoughts create themselves from the outside input that comes in. All that negativity, all the insecurities and all the things that everybody else is saying becomes the creator of your life.

Other people's opinions and the outside things that are going into your mind will create the fear, the lack of confidence and the disbelief in your self. They will create barriers that keep you stuck in your well-rehearsed, habitual rut. When outside chatter gets into the subconscious mind, it will convince you not take any chances in life keeping you from moving forward in your life. Remember, outside chatter doesn't matter.

Eventually you start to believe you can't do something because it's "to risky" or "what will everyone think if you fail?" You start living in fear and you're too afraid to do what you really want to do. If you want to reach the next level of your life financially, personally or anything, you must learn to control your mind and stop letting your mind control you.

When you get quiet and become aware of the thoughts you are thinking you must ask yourself, are these thoughts really mine or am I trying to please someone else? Am I trying to live up to someone else's expectations of who or what I should be? The moment you realize who you really are and understand why you think the way you think and accept yourself unconditionally, you will begin to understand that you really do control your thoughts. You really do control your life. You begin to consciously take control and you have the willpower to stick by your decision, because they are actually YOUR decisions.

You must be aware that with this realization comes great responsibility. You are solely responsible for your life. You must own your mistakes and accept the responsibility when things don't go as planned. Don't dwell on them, own them and move on. You may also feel that sense of accomplishment and pride when things do go right. Don't dwell on them either accept these emotions and continue to move forward.

So how would this play out in your life? It might sound like this:

All right I need to focus on my future. I want to be better at my job. I will educate myself in order to do my job better, to get a raise or to move up to a better position. Remember we become what we think about. Negative thoughts produce negative emotions. Negative emotions produce a negative future. So if you're not focusing on what you want, if you're not thinking about the things that you want in your life or you're just going through life and reacting to what happens day in day out, you're not in control of your life you are allowing life to control you.

What do you want? Who are you? What makes you happy in life? Are you doing what you really want to do? What are you doing now that you don't want to do and why are you doing it?

These are questions you must ask yourself in order to define who you are and set appropriate goals. Remember it's your life you are in control.

Okay I understand sometimes you have to work at a job that you're not happy with to make money to pay bills to pay for your house. Sometimes, people that have very expensive cars are just trying to impress people that they don't even like. Some people buy expensive watches to show off to people they don't care about. They are just fooling themselves. I see people taking a lot of money out of the bank to post a picture on Instagram trying to show how rich they are. That's all crap.

Decide what you need. What's the priority in your life and how you're going to get to where you want to go?

You must have a goal otherwise you'll never know when you reach it.

Just remember, things aren't going to happen in a week in a month in a year. It could be five years ten years. You have your whole life ahead of you do not need to rush into everything, be patient. Don't try to be successful and make a million dollars in a week or two and say I'm going to invent the next iPhone or I'm going to solve the problems of the world or cure cancer because chances are that's not going to happen.

Do you realize you can create any emotion you desire? If you sat there by yourself and thought of something very sad, you'll begin to experience the emotion of sadness. On the other hand, if you think of something that's very happy in your life, something that you love to do you'll experience the emotion of happiness. What you are doing when you do that is you are creating your emotions. You're creating your awareness around those emotions and creating your future just by what you're thinking. Don't forget your brain doesn't know if it's real or imaginary, so consequently it thinks that everything is real.

Try it some time — sit there and think of something that's very depressing for a long period of time and you'll get depressed. Later think of something that makes you very happy and BOOM, there's your proof.

All you need to know is that your mind controls your body but you control your mind, with your thoughts.

You have to be aware of what you're thinking. You have to know what you want. You have to know who you are accept who you are, good, bad or indifferent. Own it and be the person that you want to be and you'll be happy. Once you "own it" you will feel liberated. That pressure will be lifted. Then watch out because you're gonna get happy!

Isn't that what we all want? We just want to be happy. I know I want to be happy. I'm happy with who I am. I'm happy with who I was in the past and I'm happy with where I'm headed in my future. I'm just happy to be alive.

It's really that simple.

Chapter 17

Believe In Your Passion

This chapter is coming from the heart. How many times in life have you had a dream or a goal or something that you want to pursue? Usually people don't give it the attention it deserves in your mind.

Reality check, no one else cares about your passion, and why should they? It's your passion, not theirs. They have their own course they are choosing. Sometimes in your life you may be hard on yourself, or second guess yourself, and you begin questioning whether this really is worth it? Am I really doing what I want to do?

If it's your passion and people keep putting it down or don't even acknowledge it, it is often hard to keep going. The reality of it is you can't expect someone else to be passionate about you dream because it's just that, yours. So, if you're expecting support from the outside world or from anyone else, you're in for a rude awakening. You have to accept the fact that you're flying solo with your passion. Take my podcast as an example of something I wanted to do. I was on a mission, and no one else can actually do it. This is something I wanted to do. It was my dream. So, if you have something that you want to do, and you're not getting support, you can't use that as an excuse not to do it. Okay? You could easily allow the lack of support to destroy your passion. Don't let that happen!

People think I'm kind of strange for doing my Be Positive Stay Positive podcast. The first question they ask is always, "How much money do you make?" My response is I don't do this for money because my reward is helping people. The support that I get from listeners' emails, texts and the number of people listening to the show says it right there. What I'm doing is worthwhile and it is desperately needed. If you're not getting support from your family for something you want to do, you have to keep going. You have to find the strength. Follow your passion/heart.

Maybe you're so excited and so passionate about what you're doing that you want the world to know so you end up telling everybody and repeating yourself. You're seeing it grow, and seeing its effect on the world. Maybe other people are jealous of the fact that you're doing something that you love. It's your passion and you get to do what you like. They may be mad because they're not doing what they love. So they take it out on you and try to sabotage your passion. But if you're passionate about something and people are cutting you down for it, don't get negative on it. Don't give up on it. Don't let the outside in. Don't listen to the outside chatter. I've said it before outside chatter doesn't matter. But it can; sometimes it matters because of who it's coming from. If it's coming from events or from general people or the general public you can get over it, accept it, and move on. But if it's coming from someone you love, somebody in your family, or a close friend and they say they're tired of hearing about it, or they don't believe in it, then that hits you pretty hard and makes you stop and question yourself.

Am I doing the right thing? Should I keep doing this? Is it worth it? But at the end of the day, if you're happy with what you're doing and you're following your dreams and your passion, then tune everyone else out.

You have to do what makes you happy. That's just the way it goes.

That's what life is. Because if you're not making yourself happy then what's the point? I mean everybody else can be happy in their own right. You really don't have anybody else to rely on. If you're hoping to get support, if you're wanting that pat on the back, that compliment from another person who is as interested all the time as you are…good luck finding that. If you do find that you're lucky. But most of the time, other people are not going to be as excited about your ideas as you are. That is unless they're making money or unless they have an investment in it.

But the bottom line is people are not going to be as excited about your passion as you are. But don't let that take away from what you want to achieve. Don't let that destroy you passion and vision.

If you have a passion and you feel like you're all alone…guess what? You're not alone. Follow your dreams and if someone jumps on board with you then that's great. But understand flying solo with your passion is okay. Believe in yourself and don't get discouraged by what other people say because they don't fully understand your final goal. They don't know what drives or motivates you. They don't know what's going on in your head. They don't know what's making you happy. Don't let that deter you or slow you down in anyway.

Follow your dream.

Follow your passion.

Do what you need to do!

~ The Positive Perspective ~

Chapter 18

Extreme Emotions

We all know someone who has an extreme emotional reaction to just about every situation whether they're overly happy, or they get overly upset over the littlest things, or they get so angry that they can't control themselves. How do you diffuse the extreme emotions or calm them down a little bit? This topic is actually coming from a letter that I received from someone who signed it…Anonymous.

It starts off...

"How can you help someone when your hands are tied figuratively? The backstory is my older daughter was being a kid, trampling through the wooded area around the house with friends. She jumped over a creek and hurt her knee. The other kids said they saw it bend back the opposite way; she apparently hyperextended her right knee. Today, she was told one of the friends blamed themselves to the point that they inflicted pain upon themselves. So how do you help someone with those extreme emotions without stepping on the child's or the parent's toes? Again, figuratively? It kind of scares me if they're having a falling out, or they get really upset. What will the self-harming friend do with the extreme emotions? That could be kind of scary. Thanks."

Well, I don't know if I have insight, but I do have my perspective of the situation. If someone is too emotional and they blame themselves for somebody else's pain and hurting themselves is a serious issue that you probably shouldn't deal with on your own.

You can however start by talking to them and see if you can actually get through to them. The first thing is don't tell them they're being too emotional. Chances are they already know it and you telling them will not be news to them. It will only anger them. This is a great time to use one of the Do's and Don'ts of dealing with extreme emotions.

Do ask what they're feeling. Sure, they're being emotional, but there's got to be a reason behind it. You can ask them, "Why are you feeling this way?" Try to earn their trust so they feel comfortable talking to you. It might help them reflect on something that's been bothering them, and help calm and control their emotions.

Don't say, "I know how you feel" especially if you don't. If you haven't walked a mile in their shoes or shared the same experiences, you don't know how they feel. But it's okay if you don't have any idea, or if their emotions seem odd or out of control to you.

We all feel things differently. You have to understand emotions are very personal.

~ The Positive Perspective ~

When a person feels something is true, it is to them. You may not understand their emotion or why it's so powerful to them but it is and you must respect that. It's real. No one wants to feel like their emotions are problems or they don't matter.

Let them know that you care enough to listen and to help them understand the emotion. But don't pry too much. They're probably going to tell you, "You don't get it. You don't get it." But you can help if you at least acknowledge their pain, and you take the time to listen to them and be open to learning from them how they're feeling.

By doing this maybe they'll get a little bit more comfortable and let you in. On the other hand, don't get angry if they don't, even if they cry for no reason or frustrate you don't get angry, but do tell them it is okay. It's really is okay. Actually say it to them; it's a simple phrase. "It's really is okay." Sometimes they will actually take that to heart, and it will make them feel a little bit better. When someone else acknowledges that their emotions are okay, as long as you are not hurting anyone, It helps.

Don't try to combat the emotions by being logical with people who are highly emotional and extremely fired up or angry. They don't want to hear your stinking logic. Maybe they are acting ridiculous to you, but they don't want to hear that logic. They don't want you to point out the obvious in their emotional state. They can't handle it. So don't do it. Emotions aren't always logical.

Do accept them and just be there for them; listen to what they have to say and acknowledge that you may not be able to help them. Maybe you don't have the knowledge, or you don't understand, and maybe you can't help, but you are there for them. You know you can't fix it, but you will be there while they need you. You're a shoulder to cry on or a person to talk to.

Don't say it's not a big deal because it is a huge deal to them. Their emotions, which they are having difficulty controlling, are a huge deal to them. So show a little emotion for them, some compassion and understanding for what they're going through involving emotions they can't control. It can go a long way and actually help them to understand why they're feeling so upset.

So back to the letter about the girl's friend who blames themselves to the point where they inflict pain upon themselves. That's a whole different situation. I don't think I would feel safe if my daughter was hanging out with somebody who wanted to inflict pain upon themselves. I would talk to the parents and let them know your fears because that's a dangerous situation. I wouldn't try to handle it myself it because you might trigger them and possibly say something wrong; the guilt would be overwhelming for you.

So my advice is for your daughter to talk to her friend. If she's that good of a friend ask her why she would hurt herself and try to let her know your daughter wants to understand why someone hurt themselves. But that might be a good road for you to approach and talk to your daughter about it and have her talk to her friend and see if your daughter feels safe.

If you don't feel safe and you have that in the back of your mind, I would act on it and do whatever it takes to protect your family. Because once something happens, it's happened. You can't unsee what you see. You can't undo what you've done. So for me, I would protect my daughter and find out about this other person who's wanting to hurt themselves and talk to their parents. I would do whatever it takes. I don't care if the kid's not friends with me anymore. I don't care. I'm trying to protect the person. I'm trying to protect my daughter, my family.

Usually people inflict pain upon themselves for attention. So maybe show her attention another way. Maybe she's not the popular kid, but there's a lot to it. It's just not an easy answer.

~ The Positive Perspective ~

Chapter 19

Keeping Relationships Positive

I'm here to help you solve the problems of your life, I want to help you open up your mind and think about ways to be happier. To be more positive and to give you tools to combat all the negativity in the world. It's everywhere.

Let me clarify this topic is not related to me, (*love ya sweetheart*). Rather it's from a letter I got about a spouse who is a little bit upset with their husband. It happens, and it will happen again and again. Marriage is a long road. It's a marathon not a sprint. It's a full-time job. You have to work at it in order for it to be successful.

They write, how do I incorporate having a positive attitude and positive thinking and strength when I lose my patience, especially with my husband? We've been together for more than 23 years. But Sunday is football Sunday and I'm not allowed to disturb him on these days. If I do, he gets rude and nasty. He's hurtful, short tempered and just obnoxious to me. Any help is appreciated.

Well, this man obviously loves football and he gets pretty wrapped up in the game. Without knowing your whole story, I can only guess maybe watching football is his escape from reality.

It's difficult for me to just make a snap judgment without knowing the whole story, but I'm going to give it a go.

What I would do if I was in that situation is approach it like this. You've got a four-hour football game. Your husband has made it clear he wants to be wrapped up in the game…totally immersed in it and doesn't want to be disturbed. Now, you can approach the situation two ways. One, you can get mad and upset and try to force your way into his zone, that part of his life where he wants to be isolated. Or two you can use that as you time.

Wouldn't it be nice to say to yourself, I've got three or four hours to do whatever I want. I'm going to leave and go hang out with my girlfriends, do a craft or take a walk. You could just hang out with the kids, or maybe just take a bath.

Now, if he asks what you're planning on doing, tell him you got your thing and I got mine. This is our personal time. It's a partnership. You have to work together. So if he wants to watch the football game alone you can do something for you; make this your time.

This is a golden opportunity for you to really do something that makes you happy.

Find something that you want to do that you don't get a chance to do because you and your husband are often together. I am fortunate that my wife and I happen to like the same football team, and that happens to be just the opposite of your situation. We love the time together and it helps that we're rooting for the same team. We really get into it. For those four hours it's just the two of us engulfed in the game that we're watching; the game of the week.

So think about that. Think about that the next time BEFORE the game starts have a talk with him. Explain that this is a perfect time for both of you to do something for yourself.

So enjoy your time. Because sometimes in marriage, you get too close too often and it gets a little irritating and you need your space. You need that space to reboot and rejuvenate your relationship. So give him the space with the football. Do what you want to do and enjoy your life and be happy.

Chapter 20

Digital Friends vs Real Life

Friends, friends, and more friends. What's so important about friends? I'm not talking about Facebook friends, or Twitter friends, <u>real friends</u>. People you can talk with. People with whom you can share your life with who you can bounce ideas off of, actually communicate with. Those are real friends

Back when I was a kid we didn't have technology. (I almost said back in my day… That was close.) I had friends and I went outside and played with my friends. Your mom would say, "Go play with your friends" you know, and that's what you did and you learned how to interact with other people. You learned how to be a person. You learned how to treat people. You got your feelings hurt. You got happy. You met a girlfriend or boyfriend. You broke up, and you learned. All this stuff is part of life, and I think kids today are not really experiencing this part of life because of all the technology; they don't have real-life friends. Many people today are basing their life on how many Facebook friends they have, how many "likes" they get on Instagram or how many followers they have on Twitter. None of that really matters. It really doesn't matter unless you're monetizing it and it's your job.

Making a living from it is one thing, but these kids and adults too who are just focusing on just getting the most people to like them online is no good. The sad thing is, most of the people online aren't the people you think they are, right? Most of the stuff people posts on Facebook doesn't reflect the real them. They don't post when they wake up in the morning and they look like crap, or when they do something wrong or bad, or the worst part of their lives. It doesn't get posted.

All of the happy stuff, all of the good stuff, is not reality. It may be a green screen behind them and then they photo shop themselves into the Riviera and say, "Look at me...I'm on vacation." What is it really going to accomplish if you're not being real?

The more we do that, the more we create a digital version of ourselves, the more we isolate ourselves from real people, from those real tangible relationships, the more problems we're going to have in the world. The actual face-to-face communication occurring in the world today is getting less & less. We need human contact to grow as people. You can never replace the feeling of human interaction because you can feel the energy. You can't get that virtually.

My real life comes first. Everything else takes a back seat until my real life is fulfilled, until I have time with my family. We always have dinner together, it's our most important meal. It's during dinner when we get the most laughs, the best conversation and feel the energy of love.

I do believe the online medium is a great way to advertise or connect with people. Since so much of everybody's life is connected to the internet and through computers you have to be a part of it. You can't let it take over your life or you may forget who you really are. If you start believing who you've created online, if you'll get lost in the fake persona you have created.

You've seen stories about gamers that play for so long they don't eat; they lose weight and get sick or actually die behind the game because they never got up. That's just crazy; it's just insane. How can you be happy when you're sitting behind a screen all the time without human interaction?

I spend a lot of time behind my screen, but I'm not being hypocritical. I'm creating a show that's worthwhile and helpful to people. Maybe it's my therapy. When you believe in yourself and you strive to connect with people in real life, outside your door, away from the screen, and you look up from your phone, or your iPad, or your computer, you realize there are real people out there, you may just find your happiness.

Sometimes people don't like what they see because of what society has become, so they retreat to the safe little world that they have created for themselves. They go back to their cyber world where they can talk to their friends as though they're real. They create a game Avatar as whatever they want, and then can be whoever they want in the game. A 90-pound sickly weakling in real life could be the hero in a game and save the world. When you get lost in that fantasy world — when it takes over your life you're not really living **your life**.

I've always thought that computers were cool from the first time I got turned on to them back when they first became mainstream. A friend of mine gave me a Wang 386 computer that would actually talk, and it was just freaky. I took this giant box on the road with my band; we'd set it up after a gig and just have fun with that little dot matrix printer (BEEP, BEEP, BEEP); it was great. It was the beginning of artificial intelligence, and I've been hooked ever since. What computers can do is phenomenal. Now with quantum computers evolving, computing is going to be unbelievable.

Hopefully, society does not become a world of introverts working behind screens ceasing to experience human interaction. It's pretty sad when you think about it; think back to Andy Griffith and Mayberry RFD. Back in the old days having fun meant fishing, camping, or hanging out with the family. You would ride bikes or build a fort. Then you get older, and before you know it you're in high school, and you have a girlfriend, and you're in the band, in a club or you're on the football team. Afterwards you go hang out with your friends and talk about good times.

Then you go to college and you say, "This sucks or this is great." You become involved in all kinds of stuff and you build relationships with all of your friends. I was in Drum & Bugle Corps. We practiced all year long and toured all summer long; those 128 people in the corps became my family and still are today. There were no cell phones or anything like that. There was no instant sharing of every detail of your life. You had to find a pay phone to call your parents and tell them what's going on. There were no videos of anything unless you had a huge video camera. There was no way to record or document activities, so you actually lived in the moment, and there's something to be said for living in the moment and not

~ The Positive Perspective ~

focussing on capturing it for the future. You might be videoing a concert with your phone and trying your hardest to get the best footage so you can watch it later, but the sad thing is… you're missing it when it's live because you're so worried about recording it you can't enjoy the moment. Don't miss out on the moment because you'll never get that feeling back watching a video.

Your friends are there, you're there, everybody's videoing saying, "Oh this is great, this is great." You get home and you watch it again saying things like, "Oh, yeah I remember we did that." Then you post it and say, "Oh I was at this concert." I think many people are missing the point, you know? I can't imagine being a national act, being an artist, being on stage looking out and seeing 5,000 phones up in the air and pointing at me. I would be thinking, "Why don't you watch and enjoy my damn show?"

So what are you going to do? If you don't get on board you get left behind. If you don't have the latest technology you can't keep up. If you don't update your computer you can't do certain things that other people are doing. Balance is the key.

There's something also to be said for people who are living off the grid. People who cut their ties with the electric company, the water company, the cable company; they use solar power and all other sources of renewable energy. They live off the grid and go back to the old style of being real and living off of the earth, becoming a farmer and growing their own food, connecting with their family and talking about what's really important.

With all that being said, I think we're losing touch with reality. We're losing touch with people. It's hard for some people to even talk to other people because they are not used to being around humans. They are only accustomed to being on the computer and texting; it's sad that society is going in that direction. But I am not totally going in that direction. I won't do it. I promise I am going to stay real. I will always put my family and people first, as everyone should. I will post things to try to keep up. I love sharing things with the world because that's who I am.

I hope the words I say trigger something in your life to make you more positive. You can always find something good in every situation, whether good or bad. You can always learn something.

My father used to say,
"You can always learn something from someone.
You can learn what to do or what not to do."

And if you think about that, that's a great phrase because this applies to every single person you know or meet. You can learn what to do to be better, be like that person, or you learn what not to do because you don't want to be like that person.

But the main thing is to be you, be true to yourself, be happy, and try to stay happy. And above all, Stay Positive.

Chapter 21

Remain In The Present

I want to give you five ways to help you remain in the present. Focusing too much on the past or worrying about your future while neglecting your present causes you to miss out on the good stuff. If you're not focusing on the present then you're not living in the moment. So I want to give you five ways to remain in the present.

The first one is to make a solid commitment to yourself to remain in the present. What do I mean?

When you get up in the morning look into your own eyes in the mirror and say: "I am going to enjoy every moment as it is happening right here in the present. I want to live for the moment. I don't want to worry about the past things I cannot change. I don't want to instill fear in my mind about the future because it hasn't happened yet. I want to live in the moment. I want to experience the happiness of this moment and the next and the next and as they come."

You have to make a solid commitment to remain in the present. You have to actually think about remaining in the present and resist thinking about the past throughout the course of your day. Are you thinking about something negative that happened in the past? Make that commitment to remain in the present.

Next, remember to have a system to remind you to remain in the present. How do you do that? Start with your smartphone. Set an alarm for every half hour or every hour. When it goes off ask yourself what you are thinking about right now? Are you thinking about the past or the future? Or, are you in the present? When that alarm goes off it makes you reflect on what you're thinking about and reminds you to be in the present moment, to experience life as it is happening. So let that alarm be a trigger to remind you to think about what's going on right then.

Number three, meditate. Everyone recommends meditation. You can meditate in your own way. Even if you're at work, close your eyes for a couple minutes and just breathe in and out. Nice and slow while you review what you're thinking about for that moment and re-center yourself in the present. Start by thinking about your body. Think about it from your head all the way down to your toes. What are you feeling? Are you feeling any aches and pains? Are you uncomfortable? Are you hungry? Are you sad? What is it? Think about it because your body will tell you what is wrong with you. Listen to it; meditate and think about how your entire body is feeling and be aware of what you are doing at the time. Right then so you can actually get back into the moment and not miss out.

Number four. Be aware of your surroundings. See what's going on around you. Don't miss out on things that are happening at the present time because if you're thinking about the past or focused on the future, you're going to miss things that are going on around you right now. Become aware of what you are thinking about at the present time. You do have an influence on what is going on around you by the way you act and the energy you emit. So think about what's going on in your head, in your body, and be aware of your surroundings. That will help you get back to the present if you've started dwelling on the past or the future, both of which you cannot control.

Number five is a biggie. Be aware of your thoughts. I say this a lot. Think about what you're thinking about. Are you thinking about tomorrow? Are you thinking about what you're going to have for dinner, or are you thinking about that vacation that's two weeks away?

Are you thinking about the past or future or are you thinking about what's going on right now in the present? Are you in the moment? Are you paying attention to your surroundings and your thoughts and everything around you so you can make proper decisions?

What are you thinking about? I'm asking you right now, what are you thinking about right now?

So there you have it. There's five ways to remain in the present, make a solid commitment to remain in the present, have a system like alarms on your phone to remind you every half-hour or hour to get back to the present, take time in your day to meditate and focus on what you're thinking about and become aware of your surroundings so you know what's going on around you and be aware of your thoughts. Think about what you're thinking now.

I've got a bonus one for you; it's a pretty simple bonus way to remain in the present. Make an effort to enjoy where you are right now. If you're standing in line at the grocery store or you're in line at the bank or you're waiting in traffic make an effort to enjoy where you are right now. Don't worry about being in traffic for 20 minutes. Use that time positively to think about something. Listen to a positive podcast or a watch positive video or think about something that makes you happy. Don't miss out. Just look around and appreciate everything. Be grateful for the flowers. Be grateful for the sun. Show gratitude every day. There's always something to be grateful for. The world is a magnificent, beautiful place. The miracle of life is all around you. If you appreciate it and live in the moment and you're experiencing the present time you will be happier and healthier.

So take the time to take inventory of yourself, of your body, of your mind, of your environment, of the people you seen most of your time with and what is happening right now. Remain in the present. Be happy. Be positive. Share the positivity. Show the gratitude. And think about what you're thinking about!

Chapter 22

Keeping A Positive Mindset

It can sometimes be difficult in this day and age to keep a positive mindset with all the negativity that surrounds us, especially if you watch a lot of TV, or if you listen to what other people say. So I'm going to give you a few ways to stay positive.

Let's start with number one. The best way to start off your day with a positive mindset is to start your day with a positive affirmation. Now, you hear that a lot and it sounds like a cliché. It sounds like, oh, here he goes again. But understand how you start the morning sets the tone for your entire day. Have you ever woken up late and panicked and felt like nothing good happened the rest of the day? Probably because you started out the day with a negative emotion or a pessimistic view that carried into everything else you experienced for that day. You let that control you; you let the negative dominate your thoughts so you just got more of the negative back. Instead of letting negativity dominate your thoughts, start your day with a positive affirmation. Talk to yourself in the mirror, even if you feel silly.

Say something like, "Today is going be a good day," or "I'm going to be awesome today, everything is going to go right and I'm going to enjoy it even if something doesn't go as planned, I'm still going to enjoy it. I'm going to have a great day." You'd be surprised how much your day improves if you start your day positively, not thinking about bills, work or other negative things. Start your day with a positive affirmation and a positive mindset. Focus on the good things. It doesn't matter how small they are focus on the good things. Acknowledge that you're going to encounter obstacles throughout the day; there's no such thing as a perfect day *(even though you'd love to have it)*. Things are going to happen. You're going to encounter a challenge. Focus on the benefits no matter how unimportant they might seem. For example, if you get stuck in traffic think about how now you'll have time to listen to the rest of your favorite podcast, wink wink. What if the store is out of the thing you want? Take this opportunity to try something new. I think you can always find the positive. There is always a way to look at the upside of things. So try to do that; focus on the good things.

Number two: Find humor in bad situations. I'm not talking about really, really depressing circumstances…don't be laughing at a funeral, but find humor in bad situations. Allow yourself to be happy and to find humor in whatever you're facing. Remind yourself this situation is probably going to make a good story later, and you'll be able to joke about it. Find the humor in bad situations.

Number three: There are no failures, only lessons to be learned. You must learn from your mistakes. Nobody's perfect.

~ The Positive Perspective ~

You're going to make mistakes, and you're going to experience failure in a lot of different areas of your life as well as with a lot of different people. Instead of focusing on how you failed, think about what you're going to do differently next time. Turn it into a lesson and that will help you turn your failures into lessons for the future.

Number four: Transform your negative self-talk into positive self-talk. Now, this is a big one. A lot of people talk negative to themselves. They say things like: I'm so bad at this, or I shouldn't have tried that. This never works for me. I can't leave out I'm overweight. When you're doing that, you're programming your subconscious mind. Self talk is so important.

Be aware of what you tell yourself because what you say becomes your reality.

You're not going to be in a positive frame of mind when you catch yourself thinking negatively. Stop yourself right then and replace those negative messages with positive ones. For example, if you say: "Oh, I'm so bad at this, I'm terrible at this." Change that to: "Once I get some practice, I'll be better at this." Or when you say: "Oh, I shouldn't have tried _____." Or "That didn't work out this time. I'll try it again."

Whatever you do, do not allow yourself to engage in negative self-talk because you'll start to believe it. Before you know it, you'll be totally negative and it will be difficult to escape that rut. It will become your life.

Next, focus on the present. Focus on this exact moment. Not tomorrow, not an hour from now, right at this moment that you're thinking about right now, focus on the present. In most situations, you'll find that it's not as bad as you imagined.

Most sources of negativity stem from a memory of a recent event or exaggerated imagination.

So, stay in the present moment and you'll be able to help yourself keep a positive mindset. By doing this, you won't go back to the past.

Number six. This is a good one, I like this one. Find some positive friends. Maybe your friends aren't the best for you. Maybe they're negative; maybe they're doing things you don't like or they're not the kind of people you want to associate with. You become more like the five people you hang around with the most. You start to turn into those people or act like them. So if they're negative, you need to get away from them. When you surround yourself with positive people, you're going to hear positivity. They're going to have a positive outlook. They're going to be telling you positive stories, sharing positive affirmations. All of their positive words will sink in and affect your way of thinking. That's going to affect the way you speak and the way you feel. Finding positive people to fill up your life can be difficult, but you need to eliminate the negativity in your life before it consumes you. It will suck all the life right out of you. Do what you can to improve the positivity of others, but don't let it drain all of your positivity and turn you into a negative person.

~ The Positive Perspective ~

You can increase your positive energy and keep a positive mindset but you have to practice. Constantly think positively and think what you are thinking about…you've heard me say that before.

Start going through these steps again. Give yourself some positive talk and focus on the good things. Find some humor, turn failures into lessons. Return to the positive talking and positive affirmations and looking for the good in situations instead of looking for the bad or waiting for the other shoe to drop, so to speak, or looking for the negative things that can happen. Don't think about that. Think about the good. Find your *Positive Perspective*!

This will attract positive energy back and your life will be so much better. I'm living proof of it. When you practice, it gets easier and becomes a way of life. Believe me!

Chapter 23

Becoming Aware Of Negative Thoughts

To start, let me point out a few of the ineffective ways people try to stop negative thinking. When we have negative thoughts we often try to use distractions and diversions or try to drown our sorrows with alcohol and or drugs. We tend to try to just bury them down deep and don't actually face them or handle the problems. That short-term fix doesn't actually correct the problem. Pushing your negative thoughts down, drowning them in alcohol or drugs and not facing them just makes them worse.

Think of it like this. Your thoughts are like seeds in a garden. Your mind is the soil filled with good seeds and bad seeds. Let's say good seeds are flowers and bad seeds are weeds. Whatever you water will grow right? So if you water the flower seeds, flowers will grow. The same goes for the weeds. Water the weeds, weeds will grow. In relation to your mind, your awareness of your thoughts makes the seeds in your mind grow. If you place your awareness on negative thoughts, you will experience negativity. If you place your awareness on positive thoughts you will experience positivity.

~ The Positive Perspective ~

Negative thoughts, just like all thoughts, are thoughts created in our imaginations. So when you have these negative thoughts, the truth is you're literally creating them in your own mind and making them worse. The big problem is not that we have the negative thoughts; the problem comes when you believe that your negative thoughts are true. I ask you to have positive thoughts and believe that they will come true. It works the same with negative thoughts. If you focus on your negative thoughts and believe them to be true they're going to come true as well. The universe will manifest your thoughts into your personal reality.

You have to recognize your unhealthy thinking and step back from it. Step back and realize this is not healthy, this is negative. Say to yourself, *I need to stop thinking this way and stop focusing on negativity. These are thoughts that I have created in my own mind. I control my mind.*

Self-criticism and negative self-talk is also very bad. If you're talking bad about yourself or you disrespect yourself, it will not be easy to create a positive environment. Your negativity is going to feed on itself. You must shift your thinking to positive thoughts and create new positive habits.

Stop focusing on the negative stuff and start thinking about what good stuff can happen. Remember, when you start to feel negative thoughts, shift your thinking to something positive. Put on some happy music, read a book, go watch a movie or call someone who makes you feel good. Get out of that negative state that makes you feel bad and quit reliving those thoughts in your mind. It will get worse and become more and more of a habit. When you relive your mistakes it creates feelings of shame, guilt, uncertainty, negativity, and a lack of confidence. You may also experience feelings of worthlessness which may arise when you replay the negativity over and over in your mind. Or when you replay the bad choices that you made and the wrong actions that you took; these make you feel bad.

The negativity arises when you dwell on the situation repeatedly with no real intention to learn and grow.

Instead you're beating yourself up or wishing things were different instead of accepting of things as they are. Don't focus on what's wrong with your situation; instead find something that's right with it. Negativity is just like positivity. It's just a thought tied to an emotion. It's not reality.

Here are a few questions to ask yourself about your negative thoughts.

1. Is this negative thought in any way useful or helpful? Become aware of the way you're feeling and ask yourself is this helping me? Is it useful? Your answer will probably be no it's not. It's very rare that a negative thought is useful or helpful to you in any way.

2. Is it true? Probably not. Chances are it's something you made up or you are replaying the negative thought so much in your mind that you believe it. But is it true or is it really just your mind manufacturing this negativity.

3. Is it just an old story that your mind is playing over and over again? Is it something that you're so used to living and listening to in your mind and playing over and over that it's become such a habit that you don't know how to get out of it. It's a consistent negative thought about the same thing over and over again. If it is, you need to replace it with a positive thought.

4. Does this thought help you take effective action? Does it help you to move forward in life? Does it help you to make good choices? Or is it holding you back and making you make bad choices or no choice at all.

5. Is this thought helpful or is my mind just babbling on the same old crap that it's been doing over and over again. Has the negativity become such a habit that you're not even thinking about it anymore? It's just a rerun playing in your mind over and over again.

6. What is the truth? What is the truth about what you're thinking about in your mind? What are your thoughts projecting? What is the truth behind it? Has your ego been hurt? Has your pride been hurt, or are you just sad because you didn't get your way? Are you upset because you're not where you hoped you would be at this point in your life? What is the truth behind your negative thought?

7. What do you really want to feel or create in this situation and how can you move towards that? When you're having these negative thoughts what do you really want to feel? Do you want to feel positive and happy and move in a different direction? That's where you change your course of thought by thinking where you want to go and how you want to take

~ The Positive Perspective ~

control of the situation and control your mind and move towards where you want to go.

8. How can you make the best of this situation? Now this is something that I've always done in my life.

My mom and grandmother taught me when I was young; you must always make the best of even the worst situation because something good that will always come out of it.

You might not see it right off the bat but you have to look for it or create it. How can you make the best of the situation? If you're having negative thoughts and you're depressed and you're upset how do you make the best out of it?

Get past the hurt. Get past the fear. Look for something you learned or some way to be better. There is a lesson in there... you just have to look for it and believe it.

9. Where would you be if you didn't have this negative thought?

Visualize the way you would feel if that negative thought didn't matter. If you didn't have this negative thought eating away your brain. Once you begin to really visualize where you would be if you didn't have a negative thought you'll start going to that place in your mind. You'll start feeling more positive and the negative thought will lose its energy. Remember your brain doesn't know if things are real or imagined. (More on that in the next book.) By practicing this you can slowly take control of your mind and move that negativity out the door. That's where we want it...gone!

~ The Positive Perspective ~

10. What new story or thought can you focus on now to replace the negative thought you're feeling? How can you look at it from a different perspective? Something I like to do is look at it like someone else is having your problem or is talking about the negativity that you're feeling. Now picture them talking to you about it and how they are feeling this way.

What would you tell them and how would you help them to feel better about their situation and to get themselves out of their negative rut so to speak? What advice would you share to enable them to get out of the negative hole and be positive again? How would you help a friend or a family member feel better in the same situation?

11. What are you be grateful for right now? Have the attitude of gratitude. You've heard that before. What are you grateful for? What are you happy for? There are things in your life that you are happy for even though you have this negativity that's eating away at you.

Remember what you are you grateful for in this moment and help yourself to get control of your negative thoughts.

There's no possible way to eliminate negative thoughts from our minds. The important thing is to not dwell on them. Thoughts are like seeds. Water them and they grow. The brain cares not if they are negative or positive. It knows it must nurture the thoughts you pay the most attention to. Energy goes where awareness flows.

Living a positive life takes practice. It's habit. It's repetition. At first, it's going to feel difficult. You're going to feel like you're playing pretend. When you're upset or you're negative and you're telling yourself to be positive you're not going to believe it; but you must to keep telling yourself you believe until you do believe it. Whatever you tell yourself over and over again you will believe.

There was a study done with three different people on a college campus. A person approached another person and said, "Oh, you don't look so good," or "Do you feel okay?" and the person said, "I feel great." Then a different person went up to that person and asked, "Are you feeling all right? You don't look so good." Then, a second person said, "Well you know I had been feeling a little bit under the weather but I'll be okay."

When the third person asked that same person, "What's the matter? You don't look good at all. Are you sure you're feeling okay?" The subject finally said, "No, I don't. I'm not feeling too good." Using the power of suggestion and because the thoughts were placed in the subject's mind, he started to not feel well.

So the more you tell yourself how you want to feel the more you will feel that way. It's not going to be easy at first, but find some positive triggers that will make you feel good so you forget about the negative stuff. Push that stuff out and realize that the negative that you're thinking in your mind is just a thought.

It's not a physical thing. It is a thought and <u>you control your thoughts</u>. Keep practicing positive thought replacement to replace those negative thoughts with positive ones. You can do it. It's going to take practice, but you can do it!

~ The Positive Perspective ~

~ The Positive Perspective ~

Chapter 24

Treating Friends Right

First, let's define what is a friendship? Friendships are bonds with people who are always there for you when you need them. You can confide anything in them. People you can trust. There are many different types of friends...acquaintances, friends, good friends, and true friends.

So let's begin with the acquaintances. These are the people with whom you work, people you talk to at the grocery store, your mechanic. You wouldn't normally open up to them, or share your personal feelings, but you accept them as they are.

How about friends? You communicate with them but don't share private details. You likely have many things in common with your friends. You trust them, and you enjoy their company. Good friends are the ones who stay by your side through good times and bad. You trust them; they trust you. Sharing private things is common among good friends.

Finally, true friends are the friends that you connect with on different levels. You can call them at 2 in the morning when you're upset about something or if you just need to talk. Maybe you need a ride or you just want to hang with them, maybe have a drink or whatever. Bottom line is you connect with them on many different levels. These are the people you truly trust with your secrets and innermost thoughts. You confide in them with confidence knowing they will not easily betray your trust. Friendships like this transcend space and time. True friends are there when you need them.

So how do you decide which friends to keep? First, you must realize you cannot keep 100 percent of your friends all of the time. You go through phases in life: you change, your needs change, and what you are able to give changes. As you grow, you tend to make new friends that are cohesive with your current way of life. Consequently some friends will not grow as you do; they remain stuck in the past. So what kinds of friends do you want to keep? You have to figure out what you value most from the people with whom you get along best. The ones who make you feel like you matter, they understand you.

They are your true friends, the ones you can trust with your most intimate secrets. My dad used to say you can count your true friends on one hand, and that's the truth; if you really think about it, you usually only need a couple of fingers.

What If I Have Trouble Keeping Friends?
So now you have friends, but they're not lasting friendships. Maybe you're having a problem keeping a friendship. You must ask yourself: Is it them, or is it something I am doing to push them away? What is causing this? Are you too much in their business? Are you not close enough, or are you not opening up enough as a good friend? Are you taking advantage of them? If you're having a problem keeping friendships, the only things you can control is your mind and your thoughts.

That being said, you have to think about what could be the underlying reason(s) your friendships aren't lasting. Maybe you don't trust them with your feelings, or you might not approve of the lifestyle they chose. Ask yourself: Would you leave them in your house when you leave? Would you give them a key to your house to take care of it when you go away? Would you trust them with your heart? So now what can you do to keep your friends?

Take interest in what your friends do and be genuinely interested. Keep sharing your own interests with them and if they pick up a new hobby or new interest, get excited about it with them. Maybe it's something you'll be into as well.

Keep the interactions frequent. Okay, that's probably 80 percent of the problem with friendships or with your friendships…not connecting with your friends as often as you should. You should see them or talk with them regularly to keep your friendship strong. Now there are some friendships, long distance friendships for example, where you call might call that friend once every six months or a year and you're still friends. I think staying in touch is 80 percent of the game. Touching base on their birthdays or giving them a call just to say hello, how's it going?

Sometimes there are conflicts in a friendship. Is it worth the temporary pain to deal with a problem one-on-one rather than hide it or lie to them or yourself? Yes, it is. Honesty is critical in a friendship. Deal head on with the temporary pain of hurting a friend and be honest with them. Hopefully your friendship will get past that. Manage your conflicts. It's a vital skill because it's the best of friends who are likely to hit a bump in the road but keep on being friends. So you have to be able to deal with the conflicts and understand both sides, listen to each other, and work it out just like you do in a marriage and in most relationships. Don't forget, every person has their own perspective on life and their own ways of doing things. When you are in a friendship, you have to respect each other's way of doing things.

Your friends are not a stones; they are not rocks. They're going to change, just as you will change. If you want to maintain your friendship you have to grow as friends. I've had friends for 50 years, maybe more, and I still keep in touch with them. I want to point out my friends have changed over the years and I have changed. My personality and lifestyle have changed. Many of the people I used to hang out with no longer fit into my world. A big problem in friendships is that people expect the other person to be predictable, but they're going to change just like you are going to change. So get over it and be their friend and accept them, just like they have to accept you and whatever changes you've made, to keep the friendship alive.

Look at yourself in the mirror. Analyze yourself. Ask yourself these questions. Am I a nice person? Do I respect other peoples' thoughts and opinions? Do I want to share my closest and feelings and emotions with this person? Everything may fall into place but maybe the chemistry is not there. Trust your gut instinct.

You have to be happy, content, and confident with yourself in order to emit the air of confidence, and to demonstrate you want to be a good friend.

So now I'm asking you, as you're reading this book: Put it down. Go look at yourself in the mirror... Do you like that person looking back at you? Be really honest with yourself and think about the kind of person who you really are. Now think about your friends. How do you treat your friends? How do they treat you? Do you get the same type of treatment back? Is it based on mutual understanding and mutual respect?

So work hard at yourself. Be happy with yourself. Be a friend to yourself and don't abuse your body. Don't take advantage yourself. Don't talk down to yourself. And when you like yourself and you're friends with yourself, I think your friendships will grow with other people.

Chapter 25

Put Your Past Behind You

Something happened to you in the past. Maybe you experienced a traumatic event. Perhaps it occurred when you're a child or a teenager, or in a past relationship, but something happened that you just can't put behind you. You can't move on.

How can you put the past behind you so you can move on with your life and enjoy the happiness and success you deserve? We all make mistakes. We all go through difficult times, but it's how you think about the past that controls your future. How you think about and utilize the past can be an excellent teacher and a great source of motivation, or it can interfere with your happiness and hold you back from living your best life. So how do you put the past behind you?

First, practice forgiveness. I understand it's extremely hard to forgive somebody for what they've done. But in order to get past it, you have to get over it. You have to forgive them. Whether it's forgiving yourself for a mistake that you made, or forgiving somebody else who you believe harmed you. One of the best possible things you could do to heal yourself from the past is to forgive yourself.

Holding onto anger and resentment is like drinking poison and waiting for the other person to die.

That's kind of twisted, but it is the same as holding onto the past when you continue to be angry and bitter. The only person you're hurting is you. So whatever old feelings you have, let them go. You'll feel so much better about yourself and the world around you. Just let it go.

Have the attitude of gratitude. You have to practice gratitude. Take time every day to feel gratitude for everything that is good in your life. I mean everything. Be grateful for the people who love you and who have helped you or taught you something on your journey through life. Be grateful for the roof over your head. Be grateful for your health. Grateful for the opportunities you've been given in life, for the flowers blooming outside your window and the blue sky overhead. Be grateful for the little things. Everything. The more you cultivate your gratitude, the easier it will be for you to forget about the things that have hurt you in the past. Let me say that one more time.

The more you cultivate your gratitude, the easier it will be for you to forget about the things that have hurt you in your past.

Remember to be grateful for the people who have made your life difficult. These people who made your life difficult have taught you to be strong. They've helped you to develop qualities like courage and perseverance. So make sure you develop a daily practice of gratitude. Whether it's in meditation, just walking around or just thinking whatever it is, do it for a few minutes every morning and be grateful and say thank you for what you have and do this every morning to start your day.

Next, consciously choose to remember how awesome you really are. That's a way to put the past behind you. Focusing on the failures will cripple your self-esteem. It will ruin your self-confidence. It will destroy your happiness. Instead focus on your past successes and remember how awesome you are. I'm sure there are many of them. Build your self-esteem and you will build your self-confidence.

A great way to acknowledge your past successes is to make a list. Simple stuff, big stuff, whatever it is. Make a list of all of your accomplishments, like learning to drive or graduating from high school or getting a first job or buying your first car. Those were all big accomplishments when they happened. Right? Now, once you complete your list, go back over it. Remember if you're able to accomplish all of those things in the past and as your younger self, you can achieve whatever else you want to accomplish now and in the future. If you could do it then when it was more difficult and you found a way to accomplish it, you can do it now. Let me repeat: You can do it now. Acknowledge the fact that there are plenty of accomplishments in your past to feel good about and allow that to elevate your self-esteem.

This will help you put the past behind you. Once you build your confidence and the good feelings about your past accomplishments, you will believe in yourself and believe you can accomplish things in the future.

I can't stress this enough you must put the past behind you. Yesterday is yesterday. Besides the great Beatles song, it's the past and you can't change it. So dwelling on it and thinking about what happened in the past only fires up negative energy; it is only going to hurt your health, your psychological well-being, your appetite...your everything. It's going to bring you down, make you sad.

You know what? Remember this...you can't change the past. Let me say it again: *You can't change the past.* So all you're doing is ruining your future by focusing on your past. Focus on the present. Think of what you want to do in the present. Think positive thoughts for the future and forget the past. You don't need to keep that in your heart, in your mind, or dwell on it because it's not going to change. Think about the present moment. Move forward in your life so you can be happy and have the things that you want in life and all of the things that you deserve.

So I hope this helps you to put the past behind you. Remember practice forgiveness and practice gratitude. Your thoughts determine your reality. Consciously remember often how awesome you really are.

Chapter 26

Dealing With Internal Judgment?

How do you deal with internal judgment when you are judging yourself and making yourself feel bad?

Listeners' Letter

I came across your podcast when I was feeling emotionally down and I was looking for some guidance to stay positive since I started listening to your words. I had a better outlook on life and started seeing things differently. However, there are still times that I just feel emotionally down and cannot pick myself up. I have everything I need a good job, a caring relationship and a nice home. I know I'm very fortunate to be where I am and to have what I need.

But there are just times I can't stop feeling other people are luckier than me. It might not sound logical to feel that way, however, I can't get rid of the thought of comparing myself with others and wanting what they have, either a job, relationship or other tangible things. I know you had a podcast speaking about how to deal with being compared by others. Would you be able to talk about how it is to deal with the internal judgment of comparing ourselves to others thinking?

~ The Positive Perspective ~

Great question. When other people judge you, you must shut them out and remain confident with yourself. If you are envious of other people and what they have and you're not happy with what you have, then maybe you need to get happy with what you have. Go after what you want and then you won't be internally judging yourself. You have to actually look deep inside and understand why you are not happy with what you have and not ask yourself why you're envious of what other people have. Look at what you have and what you've accomplished in your life.

You may say to yourself, OK, here's my relationship. How do I feel about this person? I mean, weigh the pros and cons, though. Do they make me smile and make me happy? Do I feel love? Do they complete me? Why am I envious of that which I don't have in my life? Then you add that to your life.

How about your job? What are you missing? Why would you envy somebody else's job? Everybody hates their jobs, right? But you have to make your life happy and do what makes you happy. I make myself happy and I like my job. I love my family. I like where I am in my life because I'm living on my terms and I'm not comparing myself to anyone else. I have created my life.

When you start comparing yourself to other people and trying to live up to other people's expectations, you are not living from your heart. You're not being who you are. You're trying to be who they want you to be and that won't that won't fly for long. Eventually you'll lose sight of who you are.

So you need to be true to yourself. You need to own everything about yourself. Crazy or nutty or whatever kind of person that you are. Own who you are.

Be that person, you'll be happier. If people don't like it, it doesn't matter. Don't envy what other people have. If you like what they have. Go after it. Not theirs, but go after your own.

If it's success, then be successful. Quit whining about it. If it's a different relationship, get out of the one you're in and start a new relationship. Don't waste your life, envying other people then dying with regret. Take that chance. Take that risk. Make the change.

Nothing's going to change until you do!

Let me just twist this around a little bit. What do you think you accomplish when you compare yourself to someone else? Do you think they're comparing themselves to you? Do you think anybody else really cares about you as an individual enough to judge you? Do they have that time? And even if they did how would it affect you? It doesn't unless you let it. Words from other people shouldn't affect you. You should be marching to the beat of your own drum.

I want you to be a strong person. I want you to believe in who you are. I want you to look at yourself, the good and the bad. If there's things you don't like, change them. Do what makes you happy, because in the end, when you're laying there on your deathbed, you want to look back and say, I had a good life, I was happy. So don't worry about what other people think. Don't compare yourself to anybody else because there's

~ The Positive Perspective ~

no one like you. It's just like that scorpion song. Remember outside chatter doesn't matter.

~ The Positive Perspective ~

Chapter 27

Rejection Sucks

Feeling rejected never feels good. Whether it's in a relationship or at a job, rejection can be difficult to deal with. You put yourself out there and you get rejected. Of course you take it personal and you think, what have I done to deserve this? What's wrong with me? Many times you place the blame on yourself. When you feel that, step back and look at the situation as an outsider. Be objective so you can figure out if it IS something you can change or if it's completely not your fault. When you do this you can view the situation from a different perspective, a positive perspective if you will. Let me explain.

Let's say you're applying for a new job. You feel as if you the most qualified. You are sure you are the best candidate for the job. After your interview you feel confident. You tell yourself you crushed it. A few days later you get the call. You didn't get the job. Mind blown right? This is where you must figure out why. Is there something you can learn to make you the best candidate next time? Did you not evaluate yourself honestly? Either way, you must own it and move forward.

OK how about being attracted to someone, expressing your feelings to them only to be rejected. When rejection comes from someone you care about, things get a lot more emotional and more difficult to overcome. The many thoughts you experience like embarrassment, anger and hurt can be devastating if you let them remain in the front of your mind. The feelings are real but just know that they are part of life. Those feelings, once controlled, become your super power. If you keep thinking about the past you get more of the past.

You have to understand how you're feeling, accept it and say, OK, I'm not going to deny the pain, I'm going to feel it, and move on.

If you've never gotten rejected by anybody in your life, then you are living way too far inside your comfort zone. You're not taking any chances. You're scared and resistant to opening up your heart for fear you may get hurt. You're not going for what you want.

What kind of life is that just living in this safe little box? You must put yourself out there and you're probably going to get rejected a few times. Don't let anyone control your feelings, or control how you feel.

Remember outside chatter doesn't matter.

Don't take it personal. A lot of times people will feel so stupid for thinking that they could have a relationship with someone. If it fails they blame themselves. They might say what was I thinking? This person is too good for me when in reality no one is too good for anyone. Why? Because we all come from the same energy so we are one. Sometimes things don't always work out as planned. What's that song? You can't always get what you want, but if you try, sometimes you get what you need. That's true in life. You can't live with negativity and dwell on that rejection. You shouldn't think that you're unlovable. You have to put it in perspective. You took a chance. It didn't work. You have to get over it and move on. It's really simple when you are in control of your thoughts and you are aware of your feelings.

Every time you dwell on anything from the past it will wear you down because you're going to be living in fear and feeling a lot of negativity. Don't let it define who you are. Don't let it devalue your self-worth.

My last thing would be to you have to learn from rejection. Ask yourself, what did I gain from this situation? What are you feeling about being rejected by this person? Let's turn the tables for a minute. I bet there's someone out there that wants to be with you but you don't want to be with them. If they pursued a relationship with you, you would say no, right? You wouldn't say yes just to be with them.

So there's someone for everyone. There's people that aren't going to get along and that's just the way it is. You take that with a grain of salt. You learn about the areas in life that you want to improve in your life and recognize that being turned down isn't as awful as you think.

<u>Now for my positive perspective:</u> Rejection can be a good teacher. It can help you to move forward and help you be smarter person about relationships. You can learn what not to do. But make sure you make it a learning experience. Turn it into a positive and move on. Don't dwell on it because it's not

going to happen. If it's meant to be. It will happen, but not if you just keep harping on it and trying to be with this person. Open your heart and your eyes to see other people and to open up and welcome a new relationship. You never know what you're missing out on. There's somebody out there for everybody. I believe it. So hopefully, you can be strong enough to get over this person.

You just accept it and say that's way it is. The earth is round. The sky is blue. Things you can't change. So just move on and move forward and think positively. Wake up in the morning and think new thoughts and new goals and new dreams with new people.

Remember, if you don't change the way you think, nothing will change.

~ The Positive Perspective ~

Chapter 28

Your Last Day On Earth

Now don't worry, I'm not going to get depressing on you here, just making an observation. I'm going to turn this dark topic into a positive, even though it seems like it's starting off on a negative. Let me tell you a little story.

It was about 2am and I was coming home from a gig. I hit a patch of ice and slid sideways in my Tahoe and was headed straight for an 18 wheeler that was sliding sideways towards me at the same time. What are the odds right? Right then so much flashed before my eyes then BAM! The left rear of my Tahoe clipped the back of the semi trailer. Luckily, I didn't get hurt.

Anyway, I got into an accident and I am okay, but I for a second there, I didn't know if I was gonna make it out of the crash alive. It really started to make me think, what if this was my last day? What if it was over? What if this was my last day on earth? I started to think about what I would be leaving behind. What's my legacy? How were people going to remember me? What impact have I made on people? I started thinking, I am so grateful for everything that I have in my life and I didn't want it to be over. So thank God it wasn't my time.

So what if it *was* my last day on earth? What would that mean? That would mean obviously no more positive podcasts. My son and daughter, be left without a father, my wife without a husband, and their lives would totally change. My friends and family would probably be devastated but in time they would go on. No one truly wants to die and most people don't want to think about it.

Maybe you've had some brushes with stupidity like I have that could have cost you your life. But they didn't. Why? You start thinking why am I still here? Why was I spared when somebody else was taken or when a child doesn't survive birth? Why am I here?

If you start really thinking about it, you'll figure out your purpose in life. I think our mission in life is to learn how to love, how to be happy and share happiness, how to be positive. So that way, when it is your last day on earth, you'll leave everyone happy. They'll be missing you, but you leave them happy. So what am I trying to say to you? I'm trying to tell you to be happy. The happiness that I feel, the wholeness that I feel, the gratitude that I feel keep me grounded.

Be aware of your surroundings and be aware of your goals and your dreams. Day to day, hour to hour be in the moment. Don't be away from your family because you're texting so much or you're on whatever app you're on or you think you have to work late because the job needs you. If you have to be away from your family, make it as minimal time as you can because every moment you spend with them is going to be so cherished when you're not around.

Some people don't get that opportunity. When you're in an accident and you have things flash before your eyes, you approach life differently. Don't let those little moments of happiness get away from you. You have to scoop them up, savor them, embrace them and remember them.

But I just wanted to ask you, what if yesterday was your last day on earth, would you be OK with that? If you're not, what would you do differently? Analyze your life and figure out what's lacking and what you want to change and start. Just start. Do it. Make the change. Be the person you want to be because you never know when you're when your time is up, when it's time to punch out, then that's it. You don't get the choice. It's always a surprise to everybody.

What can you change about your life to be a better person, to be happier, to be more communicative with your family, to be more loving, to be a better father, a better dad, a better employee, just a better person? How can you help others? Because it's all about happiness. Everything in life should be about happiness. Being successful does not mean you have a lot of money in the bank. I think that is totally wrong. I think being successful is being happy and being able to share your life with the people you love.

Find that happiness deep inside. You can do it and you can turn every negative situation into a learning experience or a positive experience.

Now, while I might have to dig deeper in my mind to figure out what came out about positive yesterday, but I am grateful that I'm still here to think about it. So that's what sets a positive right there.

Chapter 29

Success = Happiness? Not Always

If you're happy, are you successful? How do you know if you're either? Well, first of all, if you feel good and you're smiling you're probably happy. Make no mistake, success is subjective. It is different to everyone. To some people it's the "things" that show how successful a person is. They feel they must impress people by flaunting their success. To me, success it is not about having a big house, expensive watch or a fancy car. It is about waking up happy every day. It's about enjoying life and spending quality time with the people I love. All the money in the world can't replace a hug from your child or a loving smile from your partner.

So what is your success and will it make you truly happy? In this culture based on profit and earnings we've grown up to attribute success and happiness to bling, stuff and money in the bank. It's such a bad analogy. We are so brainwashed from childhood to think that success is money and things — it's not. You can be successful by being happy and content and living a good life.

You have to live within your means and create your success for yourself right. Unfortunately many of the successful and the rich people aren't very happy. A lot of people aren't really happy because they give up the real chance for happiness on their way to the top. All they're doing is working for all this money and these cars and for what? To prove to other people how successful they are. Believe it or not, many people are living this charade to impress people they don't even like. It's such a shame that they believe money is the answer to their happiness and they think that having money is the key to their happiness and their success. It is almost never the answer.

Now let's be real here, money can buy you things that make your life more fun, but if you're not truly happy inside true success/happiness will always be out of your reach.

There are people that have very little money that are living on the streets that are happier than millionaires. It's all about how you feel inside and how you share your positive energy with the world. Your perspective on life has a lot to do with it as well. So what is it that makes you happy? Are you doing what makes you happy? I don't mean with just your job but are you living the lifestyle that is making you happy? Do you go home and think I like my house. I like my family I like my life. It's not about the money. Because when the money's all gone, happiness will still be there. Right.

"Success is all the money in the world. Happiness is having people to spend it on."

So if you have all the money in the world and you've got nobody to share it with or spend it on is that is not success. And you're not going to be happy especially if you're alone. If success is measurable, happiness is limitless. If success is a fancy car, happiness is a great ride. If success is the race happiness is the finish line.

How many people actually love their job and love the work they do? Are you doing what you love? Does it make you happy to do what you do to make a living? If not why are you doing it?

Life is too short. So think about what you're doing in life. Are you striving for what other people think you should have? Are you trying to make a lot of money and drive that fancy car and pay for that five bedroom beautiful house just to impress people that you don't even like? Think about that. You're trying to impress people that you don't even like and you think that's success. That's crazy talk. All the while the people that you love are missing out on your life and you're missing out on theirs because all you're focusing on is money.

Money is not the key to happiness. So what is your success? Do you feel successful right now or are you thinking about what other people think about you?

What I'm trying to say is success is determined by you and what you want and by what you think is successful. Don't try to please other people and don't try to be someone that you're not because you won't be happy. Figure out what success means to you.

It's a great feeling when you can look into that mirror, smile and be content with where you are. In my eyes you're successful and you should feel that way too because there's not a lot of people that can actually look in the mirror and smile at themselves with content and be happy.

Chapter 30

Think Positive Everyday

What's the point in being positive in the first place? Why even bother? Why not just let life happen to you? To me, letting life just happen to me would be the same as driving a car with your eyes closed. Once you realize you actually DO have control of your thoughts, feelings and emotions, you begin to understand anger, stress and negativity just aren't worth it.

What are real benefits to being more positive? First and foremost you will be happier. By controlling your negative impulses, emotions or reactions you create less stress. Stress hormones create negative emotions that are programmed into our brains that help us survive.

Here's an example. If we came across a dangerous animal in the wild, the negative emotions of fear and anxiety would narrow our focus so all we can think about not becoming that animal's dinner. It has helped mankind survive. Of course modern life doesn't put us in life-and-death situations most of the time. That being said, if you allow your constant negative emotions to narrow your thinking, you will always living with stress. It makes you less open, makes you hardheaded and difficult to communicate with.

Your subconscious mind is not easily reprogrammed. When you say I don't want to smoke without believing it, without being emotional attached to quitting smoking, you subconscious won't believe it and will not help you with willpower to achieve it.

What does that mean? It means that we all struggle with changing our negative thoughts, feelings and habits into positive ones. The body gets used to a way of life, a life habit created by years of programming by family, media and society. It is the way you were raised and the way you've lived up to this moment that makes it very hard to change.

Positive thinking can actually improve your overall happiness. Duh right? So if you're positive it's going to make you feel happy all the time right? No! Thinking positive goes hand in hand with controlling how long we hold on to negativity. We all experience negativity in life, it's how we choose to respond to it that changes everything.

Studies have shown that being positive directly affects your physical health. So it must be true that negativity makes you sick right?

So if being negative makes you sick, shouldn't being positive make you well?

Where are you in your life? Who do you hang out with and are they actually influencing you in a positive way? If they're not influencing you positively then you something needs to change. Either they need to be on board by being positive or you need to spend less time with them or cut them out of your life completely. I have sticky notes on my computer and on my mirror in the bathroom with positive affirmations on them. If I happen to get off-track I'll have it right there n front of me, be positive.

Start smaller than you think.

Don't start with "I'm going to change my entire life in one swoop". That's crazy talk. Start with smaller things, a little change here and there, achievable tasks. Just trying to see the positive side of something and not saying oh here's what can go wrong think about what can go right and enjoy the moment.

Take note of at least one positive moment every day.

Something positive happens to you every day if you're paying attention. Be aware of your surroundings and welcome the positivity. If you write it down you can say oh there's a reason to be happy and positive. One positive moment that you take notice of can help you to gain positivity and to think positive throughout the day. A good time to think about this is when you lay down to go to bed.

Meditation and Relaxation.

Find a quiet place where you can have 5-10 minutes meditating. It is very beneficial for the mind and body. I have times when I'll get really quiet and I want to be by myself. During these times I actually listen to what my thoughts are and to listen to what I'm saying to myself. I begin to feel gratitude for everything. I analyze my thoughts and feelings making sure that there are no negative thoughts stealing my positivity. I try to do that as often as possible sometimes people think I'm dozing off but I'm actually in my quiet place in my mind. Meditation may help you to get the strength and clarity you need to be positive.

The more you fill your head with positive thoughts the better off you'll be. When you're around people that are positive, chances are you thinking positive thoughts as well. Take note of the good things in your life and be grateful for them.

You must be honest with yourself when meditating and self-analyzing. There's a point in your life when you have to actually look into the mirror, see that person looking back at you and be totally happy with that person looking back at you.

Life is about happiness. It doesn't matter what people say or if they dislike anything about you. The questions you must ask yourself are: Are you doing what's making you happy? Are you honest with yourself? Are you a loving, caring person? Are you compassionate and empathetic? Are you where you want to be in life?

If not, stare at that person in the mirror and figure out why then tell that person the truth of why they're not where they want to be or why they are not positive or why you're not happy or why you don't have the job that they want. (By the way the they is YOU.) Whatever the excuse is, you have to own it. It's all your fault. You have to take responsibility for your life, for everything that's happened to you. You are where you are in life because of the decisions you have made in the past. If you want to think positive every day you have to own your mistakes and own your successes.

As soon as you wake up it's your day. You can make it whatever you want it's your day.

If you're not focusing on being positive then your day is ruling you. It's controlling and dictating you life.

In order to have a happier life you have to take control of your life and actually think about things that you want to become. Whether it's closing that big deal, landing that big client or asking that person out on a date, as long as you have control of your thoughts and you're consciously thinking about what you want you'll be all right.

Thinking positive everyday and trying to see the good in everything doesn't come easy. When you first got on a bike you didn't hop on it and start riding, you had to practice. If you want to learn how to play the guitar you have to take lessons and learn how to play. Anything you want to be good at you must practice and do it over and over till it becomes habit.

Thinking positive works the same way. You are creating a new habit, a positive habit. It's something new that you're not used to. You actually have to work at it and if you don't work at it, it's not going to happen and you will find every excuse of why your life is miserable. But in the end the excuse is looking right back at you from that mirror.

~ The Positive Perspective ~

Chapter 31

Have You Made The Right Choice?

This chapter is something that troubles me quite a bit but I've learned to come to grips with it. How do you know if you've made the right choice? You don't know until after you've already made it right? How do you know if you're making the right choice in life whether it's a partner, a new job, where to live, whether to have children or not? How can you know if you've made the right decision? The answer is you don't. You will never know if you make the right choice until after you've made the choice.

Once you make the choice you'll recognize if you've made the wrong decision. But actually making the choice is the first tough decision to make. Making a decision is the hardest part. You have to remember that when it comes to making a decision in life you're never going to know the alternative outcome of what you didn't choose. You're never going to know the outcome because you didn't take that road. You're not going to know where that path would've taken you. So stop worrying about it and just make a decision. If it turns out to be the wrong one, change direction. Switch gears

Let's say you choose a job in Atlanta and you take that job and you also get a job in L.A. and you didn't take that one. So you take the Atlanta job things go well work and your life is going well and you know life is good and then everything's great. But what if you to take the job in L.A. and you fly out there and your plane crashes and you die. Then your life is over. You can't predict the future you can only create it. All you can do is act on your decision.

So you make the decision and if it's the right decision you win. If it's not the right one, you adjust and you change course. Make the decision, stop worrying about the perfect decision because everything in life is what you make of it. Sure you try to predict every possible outcome so you can make an informed decision. Don't dwell on it too long, make your decision and stick to it. You have to act fast. They say that success comes to people who can make decisions quickly but are slow to change them. Don't give up easily, be persistent but also be objective and accept defeat if you've made the wrong decision. There's absolutely nothing wrong with changing your mind and don't let anyone tell you there is. Many successful people realized a bad decision and changed direction, changed their mind. Steve Jobs would change is mind frequently if he thought time and effort was being wasted on something.

But how do you know if you made the right choice? Well, like I first said, it's easy to recognize when you made the bad decision or the wrong choice but how would you know if you're in the right situation?

Being patient and following through is important. But what if you have been patient and it's not right for you? How do you know when it's time to move on or change direction? Well, one of the signs is things that used to be fun are no longer enjoyable. It's just no fun and it's sucking the energy out of you. When you try to get up to go to work, you can't get motivated, you can't find anything good about it or any reason to go on? You keep asking yourself why am I here, what am I doing this for, why why why? When you start asking yourself why, why, why then I think it's time to rethink your decision and change course

Another reason another thing is the excitement of your decision say to get married, buy a new house, start a new job or to buy a new car. You're excited about that when you're thinking about making these decisions and you're thinking about oh this is going to be great.

And then the excitement turns to exhaustion you just can't even get up for that job. The excitement is turning into exhaustion because you're trying to be excited you're trying to be positive. If it's getting more and more difficult for you to remain positive in a certain situation you have to look at that situation and ask yourself should I be in this situation or should I change course? Do I need to alter my plans and try something else?

There's outcomes and circumstances that happen because of the decisions we make. There's a course of an action that you follow after you make that decision whether it's to keep moving forward and progressing or it's to change course and make a new decision. You have to just think about it and if it's not making any sense to you anymore and you can't infuse positivity into the choice that you've made, it's time to re-evaluate.

It's time to own your decision and say well I tried this. It's not working. I've got to do something else. At least you tried and followed through with your decision. That's a win. You're not going to regret not making that decision or just not make it. You know not making a decision is the worst thing you could do because you're just floating through life and letting life make the decisions for you then you're not in control right.

If you're doing something because you want to not because you have to, I think you've made the right decision.

The grass is not greener on the other side.
If it is, it's probably artificial turf.

So if you do what want to do then you've made the right decision. You can be positive and be productive and move forward in life and look forward to the next decisions. Some people really blow it out of proportion and over analyze the crap out of decision making. When they are faced with a decision they are like a deer in the headlights. They're so stuck in trying to weigh all the pros and cons of both sides of the decision for so long that either they lose the opportunity or they never make the decision at all.

You have to believe in yourself, believe in your decisions analyze both sides of the coin then make the decision. Don't waste time, You have to act fast you can't wait around. As Dr. Joe Vitale says *the universe loves speed.*

~ The Positive Perspective ~

You can't just waste time trying to predict the future because if you're looking at both sides of the decisions of a decision right and you think well if I do this could happen then this could happen and then maybe this could happen again. The scenarios that you're making up in your mind are usually being created by the fear of the unknown. It makes sense doesn't it by the fear of the unknown.

You never know what's going to happen so you're afraid to step off into the right direction because it might be wrong. If you start thinking what's the worst that could happen? You start really playing a tennis match in your head with the negativity and the fear. And guess what you get overcome by fear. You don't make the decision and you live with regret because you didn't take the decision and then you don't know either outcome because you didn't make the decision. So make a decision.

Follow it through. You're not a fortune teller. You can't predict the future. There's no time machine to go back. So make the decision follow through with it 100 percent put all your effort into it and make it happen. If it doesn't happen change course.

So if you've got a decision that's bothering you right now I want you to make that decision even if you have to write down all the options down a piece of paper to come up with it. Do it.

Chapter 32

Infinite Intelligence

Let's talk about infinite intelligence and how it affects everything that you do and how if you tap into that infinite intelligence, your life will be amazing. Where does it come from? Everything is made up of energy. Everything is vibrating at a certain frequency. It's all moving and it's all around us we just can't see it with our eyes. Energy can't be created or destroyed and it's always there. We're all infinite beings and we're connected to everything and every one.

We can tap into so much energy if we just let it happen. There's so much out there that we don't understand yet. Who knows where technology's going to take us in the future? You have to believe, just like the X-Files, you had to believe. I believe that there is an infinite intelligence that we all can tap into if we so desire. If you're persistent with your thoughts and you believe with your heart, you can make it happen. I honestly believe that you can cure yourself of diseases. You can make anything happen. A group of people working towards the same goal, become like a mastermind and make things happen as a collective.

You have so much more power when you're in a group of people and you are brainstorming. It's amazing what you can do if you put your mind to it. What's his name? Mahatma Gandhi got 2 million people to think the same thing. How do you do that and to work together? But it's the power of the mind. If you harness the power of your mind, you can have, do or be anything that you want. It's true. Where you are in life is your choice. I've said it before, but you have to really take a good look at yourself and see who you are and accept who you are and change what you don't like and really feel the energy from around you.

Now you're probably saying to yourself, Nat has lost his mind. He's lost his freakin mind. Not really. I've always thought this way. I've always thought that there is a superior being. The creator or superior being _is_ the collective, which is all of us.

We're all one giant being if you think about it, we all come from energy. Your desk, your computer, your TV refrigerator, your car, it's all the same. Everything is just vibrating differently. Energy cannot be created or destroyed. So nothing really disappears. It just vibrates at a different frequency. It's pretty freaky when you start thinking about it like that, you know? And here we are. We're here on this earth for a reason. You're put here to learn something. To learn show to love unconditionally.

This is just a small part of your infinite journey. Some will take advantage of it and try to learn as much as they can. Live is truly incredible. The emotions we can experience, the joy we can create, the abundance we can manifest. It's all within your reach if you just open you mind and believe.

And if you can share it with someone else, that's even better. But you have to learn how to love yourself first so you can love other people. What's that song? All we need is Love by The Beatles.

This is why we are here. We are all part of the collective infinite intelligence, we're all trying to learn how to love and how to coexist because we're all one. But this part of your journey, this life, you need to make something of it, you need to learn how to love.

So take a long hard look at yourself and ask yourself am I doing everything I can to get what I want in life? It's that that simple. If you're not then face it, own it, and take control of your mind.

I've done it.

Now it's your turn.

You can do it!

Printed in Great Britain
by Amazon